Take Intelligent Risks GIVE BACK
PLAN SURROUND YOURSELF WITH WINNING PEOPLE
Question RECOGNIZE OPPORTUNITY
BREAK RULES TAKE INVENTORY
Take Intelligent Risks GIVE BACK
PLAN SURROUND YOURSELF WITH WINNING PEOPLE
Question RECOGNIZE OPPORTUNITY
BREAK RULES TAKE INVENTORY
Take Intelligent Risks GIVE BACK
PLAN SURROUND YOURSELF WITH WINNING PEOPLE
Question RECOGNIZE OPPORTUNITY
BREAK RULES TAKE INVENTORY
Take Intelligent Risks GIVE BACK
PLAN SURROUND YOURSELF WITH WINNING PEOPLE
Question RECOGNIZE OPPORTUNITY
BREAK RULES TAKE INVENTORY

SECRETS OF A RUTBUSTER

Breaking Rules and Selling Dreams

For Michael
who must be a rutbuster!
MJD

SECRETS OF A RUTBUSTER

Breaking Rules and Selling Dreams

MYRA JANCO DANIELS

Myra Janco Daniels

RUDER FINN PRESS

Editorial Director: Susan Slack
Creative Director: Lisa Gabbay
Senior Art Director: Sal Catania
Art Director/Designer: Diana Yeo
Production Director: Valerie Thompson
Digital Imaging Specialist: Steve Moss

ISBN 13: 978-1-932646-49-8
ISBN 10: 1-932646-49-3
Printed in China

Dedication

To the many people who let me know they cared – and who helped me bust out of the ruts in my life.

TABLE OF CONTENTS

Introductory Note *by Muriel Siebert*

Myra Daniels is a dreamer. Unlike most dreamers, however, Myra is also a doer. She is a woman who turns dreams into action and makes them come true. She has done this many times in her life.

Before moving to Florida, Myra was president of the Draper Daniels advertising agency in Chicago. She had a very successful career in advertising, becoming the first woman to head a national ad firm.

She moved to Florida with her husband for what seemed like an early retirement. But when her husband died, Myra took a closer look at her community and she began to dream, and to wonder how she could make it better. The region's main cultural activity at the time was a young volunteer orchestra which performed in local high schools. It needed help, particularly with fundraising.

Myra went into action. She conceived the plans and raised the money to take the orchestra to new levels and to build it a permanent home – the Philharmonic Center for the Arts, in Naples. She booked the performers, raised the cash and ran the Philharmonic Center like a business. Eventually, the orchestra and the arts center she created became nationally recognized.

Some people would have stopped there – but not Myra. She dreamed and acted. Ten years after the Philharmonic Center opened its doors, she started the Naples Museum of Art, the region's first full-scale art museum. Today, the orchestra, the Philharmonic Center and the Naples Museum of Art are all successful ventures – not only artistically but also financially.

Major developments like these do not happen by accident. Myra's vision and determination enabled the creation of a major cultural center, which brings much enjoyment to people's lives. Myra's life and career provide many valuable lessons. I am honored to provide this introduction.

Muriel Siebert
President, Muriel Siebert & Co., Inc.
First woman to own a seat on the New York Stock Exchange

INTRODUCTION

"Something wonderful has happened."

With those words, we cut the ribbon and opened the doors to the Philharmonic Center for the Arts on November 3, 1989. With its blend of parapets, spires and Palladian columns, the center – comprising a performing arts hall, four art galleries, a black box theater and two sculpture gardens – resembled "an elegant, green, modern-day castle," one reporter noted, an anomaly in the sleepy, residential community of Naples, Florida.

Those who stood in the glittering hall that evening shared an excitement – the excitement of having built something from nothing. Three years earlier, this cultural center was just an idea – and not a very realistic one, in many people's estimation. Now it was open for business, ready to welcome such top-drawer talents as Itzhak Perlman, Rudolf Nureyev, Frederica von Stade and Bill Cosby to a community where for decades the only performance venues had been churches and school gymnasiums.

First Lady Barbara Bush flew into town that day to tour our complex. Journalists from several national media organizations came to report on the opening. What our community had built was unusual, and newsworthy, for several reasons. First, we were inviting world-class art and entertainment to a region considered by some a cultural backwater, a community perhaps best-known for its annual "swamp buggy" races. Second, this $21 million arts center was built almost entirely through private donations, gathered in an intensive grassroots fundraising campaign. And, finally, the Philharmonic Center was the only arts complex of its size in the country to combine the performing and the visual arts, to present marquee stars from the worlds of classical and popular entertainment along with museum-quality art exhibitions and a resident orchestra.

As we gathered in the hall on opening night, I thought back to other times in my life when I had shared the excitement of building something from nothing. At age twenty-four, for instance, I started a little two-person advertising agency in Terre Haute, Indiana; a year later, we had ten employees and were doing a million dollars in business. There were others as well, which I'll talk about in this book.

If I have a talent, it's for believing that virtually anything can be accomplished when people have faith in themselves and their ideas – and then helping them turn those ideas into tangible results. I love to see other people realize their potentials – and am saddened when they fall short. I sometimes think of myself as a baton twirler more than as a businesswoman.

When I was a young girl, my grandmother used to tell me "You can do it." I was naïve enough to believe her, and those words helped me accomplish things I didn't think I could do. When I realized how powerful those four words could be, I said them to others and discovered a real-life way of making dreams become reality.

When we began to envision our arts center in Southwest Florida, there were many skeptics. Some said we were trying to force big-city culture on a region that wasn't ready for it. Vituperative letters appeared in the newspaper accusing us of "ruining" the community. Several times I received threatening phone calls in the middle of the night. "Get real," I was told. "You're talking pie in the sky." "You're dreaming."

They were right about the last part. We *were* dreaming. But more than that, we were selling a dream, a dream that the public ultimately bought. Each year since 1989, our cultural complex has grown. We now present more than four hundred events a year and feature a nationally recognized resident orchestra, which is rated among the most fiscally sound in the United States. In 2000, we added a $12 million, three-story art museum to our complex, which has exhibited work by artists ranging from Picasso to Rauschenberg to Frankenthaler. Started with nothing, our arts complex is now a $105 million corporation.

If we had heeded the warnings of the skeptics, none of this would have happened – and our community might have been very different.

Much of my career was spent in the advertising business, where for years I honed the art of selling. To some people, the idea of "salesmanship" has negative connotations, associated with telemarketers, TV commercial jingles and spam e-mails. I think of it more broadly, though, and positively. Whether we realize it or not, we are all salespeople, trading in values, talents, beliefs and ideas. Often the product we are selling is ourselves. In these pages, I'll encourage you to redefine "salesmanship" – along with other concepts such as failure, success and risk-taking.

One of the things I like to sell people on is "rutbusting" – breaking out of the ruts in our lives that keep us from our true natures, from our singular passions and talents. The main reason people fail to achieve what they want in life, I believe, is simple: They get stuck. Stuck in their routines, stuck in their thought patterns, stuck in their social circles, stuck in their doubts and their fears of the unknown. Most people don't realize how easy it is to change this – to replace negative habits with positive ones, and to become unstuck. Many people don't even *recognize* the ruts that prevent them, over and over, from reaching their potentials. Because so much in our culture encourages us to live in our "ruts," many people don't even think about the alternative.

The first time I came across the term "rutbuster" was in a business book by Auren Uris titled *The Executive Breakthrough*. This was in the late 1960s. To my surprise, the author was using the word to describe me. I had recently won the National Advertising Federation's "Advertising Woman of the Year" award and had become the first woman to head up a national ad firm. Mr. Uris included a chapter in his book on me – labeling me a "Rutbuster."

At first, I didn't like the sound of it. But in time, I came to understand and appreciate the meaning of this word – and to apply it to my own approach to business and to life. As I began writing this book, I took a hard look at my life – at my mistakes and failures as well as my successes – and tried to answer this question: *What are the most important lessons that I have learned?* Then: *How can I pass these along to others?* I boiled these lessons down to eight ideas. I call them "secrets," because they were secrets to me until I was able to identify them; but they're really lessons, the most important things I have learned in the Big Classroom – lessons that I could have used when I was starting out in business, and at many pivotal points throughout my life. I have woven these eight "secrets" through the book.

In the weeks after the tragedies of September 11, 2001, I talked with many people who were re-examining their lives and their priorities – turning or returning to more fundamental concerns. Surveys showed that interest in religion and volunteerism soared in those weeks. Unfortunately, surveys also showed that for most people this reaction did not last beyond a few months. The response to September 11 says a lot about our make-ups – too often, it takes difficult or tragic circumstances to force us to see clearly, to recognize the value of our day-to-day lives and to begin living in a way that is commensurate with that value.

This book tells my story; but it's really a story about belief and how it can be used as a tool to change lives. I hope that – at least in a small way – it helps you to achieve some big things in your life.

ONE

The Adventure of Being Different

"Security is mostly a superstition. It does not exist in nature . . . Life is either a daring adventure or nothing." – Helen Keller

My first mentor stood just four foot eleven, but she was a giant in other ways. Her name was Sophie Jancowitz, and she was my grandmother. At a time when women were expected to stay home, cooking and cleaning, my grandmother hung out her own shingle – S. Janco Real Estate (S. because she believed that people would not have walked in if she called her business Sophie Janco Real Estate) and became a successful broker. For a while, my father worked for her.

Sophie decried what she considered an overabundance of "me-too-ism" in the world. She had some firm, if unorthodox, convictions about how her son's daughter should be raised and, at times, butted heads with my mother, who was far more traditional. Mother told me what other mothers told their children: Listen attentively to adults and speak only when asked a question. My grandmother said:

"If you have an idea, don't be afraid to express it." Having to choose between such contradictory advice, I often sided with my grandmother – mostly because of the surprising places our alliance took me. My grandmother showed me that with a little courage, I could do things I never imagined I could do. She urged me to be different, to take risks and to recognize opportunities. Most importantly, she lent me a perspective: Life should be an adventure. Don't accept everything you're told. Life is made of rules, but some rules are meant to be broken. A lot of my character as a child was cast in the mold of Sophie Janco.

My grandmother didn't harbor illusions, though. She knew that life wasn't easy or fair, and she endured a number of failures and disappointments. But even when circumstances were difficult for us, as they often were during the Depression, Sophie showed me – largely through her example – to look at life as an adventure. I haven't stopped doing that. That is the first important lesson I learned because it puts the others in perspective.

My earliest memory is the smell of onion soup and the voices of immigrant men in our living room, speaking to one another in their native languages. I was four years old, coming in from playing in the rolling sand dunes near our home in Gary, Indiana.

It was my grandmother who brought the immigrants into our home. Sophie was an immigrant herself, who arrived in this country from Bucharest when she was nine years old. She married at the age of fifteen and had two children, the first of whom was my father. Although her formal education ended with grade school, Sophie had a passion for learning that burned throughout her life. Eventually, she taught herself nine languages.

I remember my grandmother as a pretty woman with snappy brown eyes and beautiful skin, who wore tweed suits and Queen Mary turbans. As she grew older, her expression changed, reflecting the hard life she had led. Sophie enjoyed

SECRET ONE

Savor the Adventure of Being Different

"To be yourself in a world that is constantly trying to make you something else is the greatest accomplishment." – Ralph Waldo Emerson

Learn to embrace the adventure of being different and your life will be infinitely more interesting and rewarding.

Our culture inherently discourages this. From an early age, we're taught to "fit in," to do "what's right" and "what's expected" – directives that keep many of us from discovering our true passions and talents.

The distinction I draw is between finding your place in life and finding your path. Most people seek out their "places": positions of respect, status and comfort. The most creative, successful and content people I've known have all thought in terms of their "paths." They have learned to follow their passions wherever they may lead.

It's a simple but fundamental difference. Most rules exist to reaffirm the status quo, not to help you reach your potential. When people expect you to do things one way, try them a different way. Teach yourself to take creative detours. Learn to listen to your own thoughts. Don't be afraid of being different. We all are.

helping people, and showed me at an early age what seemed a strange human alchemy, a form of white magic – how by helping others, we could feel better about ourselves.

This was the 1930s, a time when hundreds of immigrant men were pouring into Gary to work in the steel mills. Many had left their families behind in Russia or Czechoslovakia or Romania and journeyed to the United States with dreams of a better life. The reality was that life here was tough, too. My grandmother understood that, and made it her mission to ease their burdens. Most of these men were poor and barely spoke English. Sophie befriended them, fed them, found them places to live and struck a deal with them – if they would learn our language, she would learn theirs.

The immigrants became like an extended family to us. I would often sit with them in our living room and they would tell me stories in broken English about the Old Country, about their families in Eastern Europe and about their own childhoods. My favorite was a Russian man named Bukar, who put me up on his knee and asked what I had done that day. When he first began visiting our house, Bukar could not speak a word of English. But my grandmother taught him our language and he eventually went on to work as a mill supervisor.

Grandmother urged the immigrants to become American citizens so that they could vote and be heard. It didn't matter to her what your politics were; the important thing was that you participate. She believed in the American Dream, in the opportunities that this country offered, and thought that everyone had a responsibility – not just a right – to pursue those opportunities.

I never thought of us as poor – even when we were – because we always had books and music in our house. I remember nights when we would create our own gypsy music ensemble in the living room: mother would play the piano and sing while my father played violin and I jumped around and banged the tambourine.

My sense of what a community can do when it works together probably has its roots in this period – in the simple pooling of food and household supplies. The

Depression was often a time of creative detours. My grandmother rented property to farmers who sometimes could not afford to pay rent, for example; when that happened, she would let them pay with the crops that they grew. For a while, we had so many onions in the house that I never had to ask what was for lunch – I just knew: onion soup. Every time I came in from playing it seemed that the house smelled of onion soup.

For the first seven years of my life, I was an only child and, for the most part, a happy one. I spent a lot of time with adults, who treated me more as another grown-up than as a child. In those days, many children ate dinner apart from their parents, but our family always shared meals – my father, mother, grandmother and myself. Every evening at the dinner table, my parents would talk about their day, my grandmother would talk about hers, and then my father would look at me and say, "Well, Myra, what did you do today?" So I had to make sure I had something to report.

My grandmother encouraged me to be enterprising, and to find ways of entertaining myself. It wasn't difficult. I spent a lot of time wandering through the Indiana sand dunes, building castles, exploring, daydreaming. The dunes were a wondrous world for a small child, full of mystery and legends. The most famous legend was "Diana of the Dunes," a beautiful woman said to resemble the ancient Greek goddess Diana. Supposedly, Diana had once lived as a hermit in those dunes and people still claimed to see her ghostly figure, walking naked through the sand.

There were beautiful tall oak trees in the dunes and I would gather acorns and string them together to make necklaces. Sometimes, I would collect leaves, dry them, put them on paper plates and then shellac them. Whatever I did, I'd report on it that evening at the dinner table.

I remember my mother and father as a loving couple, who almost never had a cross word for one another – at least not in front of me. They complemented each other well. My father was a simple man – gentle and quiet – with big brown eyes.

SECRET TWO
Master the Art of Giving

There are many intangibles in life – many forces we deal with every day that defy simple explanation. One of the most important of these, I have learned, is the relationship between giving and personal fulfillment.

Winston Churchill said it well: "We make a living by what we get, we make a life by what we give."

Giving can be many things. It can be simple words of encouragement; a donation to a worthy charity or cause; a surprise gift to a loved one.

Unfortunately, this is often an overlooked factor in the equation of personal and business success. I can't fully explain it, but I know it works. Giving creates a positive energy that not only makes us feel good about ourselves, and others, but it also enables us to see solutions to problems and to break out of the ruts in our lives.

There is a correlation between giving and success and between giving and contentment. But this correlation is complex, and something of an art form. It takes time to understand and to master it. Generosity is a source of energy and inspiration. Learn the art of giving, and you'll be surprised what you get.

His name was Elias, although everyone called him Al. My mother, Cecilia, was more outgoing. Before she married my father, Ceil – as everyone called her – had worked professionally as an opera singer.

My parents understood and accepted the responsibilities of raising children. They never just parked me with a babysitter – in fact, I can't remember ever having a babysitter. We often did things as a family – bobsledding, visiting the museums in Chicago, going on long walks.

But the biggest influence on me was always my grandmother, not my parents. Sophie gave me a lot of love and encouragement during my early years. She wanted me to accomplish things, and to make my own path, as she had done.

Although she was the least educated member of her family, Sophie was in some ways the smartest. Her brothers and sister were given opportunities in education she never had, one of them graduating from Harvard. My grandmother was smart in more practical ways. I don't mean to paint her as a saint. Sophie had problems like everyone else, but she also had the confidence to overcome them. At age fifteen, she married a man in retailing who was ten years her senior. It was an arranged marriage, and one she resented. They never divorced and stayed pleasant to each other through the years – mainly because of the children – but they lived separate lives. Sophie's second child was Ruth, although we sometimes called her "The Tumor." There was an eighteen-year gap between my father's birth and the arrival of Ruth. As my father told it, Sophie announced one day that she had a tumor and, not trusting Indiana doctors, she took the first train to New York to have it examined. The tumor turned out to be my Aunt Ruth.

During the Depression, Sophie struggled and failed in business like many other people. But she always dusted off her Queen Mary turban and went right back out swinging. Sophie wanted me to be that way, too. It was my grandmother who taught me perhaps the most important lesson of my life, although it took me years to understand and appreciate it.

Party Favors

My first business lesson came at the age of four. My grandmother surprised me one day by asking if I'd like to start my own company. "I'll help you," she said. "What business do you want to go into?" I thought about it a while – until lunch – and then told her, "Party Favors." I loved colors and I loved parties and figured that I could make paper hats and candy baskets that would be used at parties.

Sophie agreed to become my first financial backer, lending me rolls of pennies to get my business going (charging two cents interest for every hundred). At dinner that night, I announced that I was now president of Janco Party Favors.

I was sitting at the dining room table later, cutting up colored construction paper, when my father walked in and looked at what I was making. "Why would anyone want to buy that?" he asked. "And who will you sell them to? You don't even go to school yet."

I got up from the table and left the room to think about it.

What he was telling me was that I needed a plan. So I went to Sophie and she gave me some advice I've never forgotten: "Create something that people want and need and you'll be successful."

So I came up with a plan: I would make paper hats and candy baskets and sell them for a penny apiece to the parents of children who were having birthday parties. If I put fudge in the candy basket, I could charge an additional penny.

My grandmother gave me a ledger to track my sales. On one side, I wrote "Make" in black crayon and on the other "Spend" in red crayon. Then I began to create the party favors from multi-colored crepe paper.

But there was still the question of to whom I would sell them. My solution was to hire Hedgewood, a little six-year-old boy from the neighborhood. Hedgewood was already in school, so he had the connections I needed. Hedgewood could find out when the children's birthdays were, and then together we could call their parents and sell our products. I offered Hedgewood the vice-presidency of the company along with a salary of ten cents a week. Hedgewood accepted. He did not yet know that I was paying myself twenty cents a week.

My father died long ago, but his questions still resonate in my thoughts all these decades later. I heard my father's questions when I started my second business twenty years after Janco Party Favors. And I still hear them today. What they taught me were the basic cornerstones of business success, lessons so simple that many business people take them for granted. Always ask the simplest question: *Why would anyone want to buy that?* The honest answer may require changing your viewpoint, seeing your product through another person's eyes. *Is this something people really want and need?*

When I entered the first grade, my grandmother offered me an allowance of fifty cents a week – a lot of money in those days.

"Now how much of it are you going to give away?" she asked, after dropping it in my hand.

"None of it," I said.

Sophie took the 50 cents back.

"You think about it. Tomorrow we'll talk again."

Some of the kids in my class came from poor families that could not afford allowances for their children. My grandmother, I realized, wanted me to give some of mine to kids who weren't so fortunate. At first, that didn't make sense to me. I didn't yet know what my grandmother knew. This was the white magic I mentioned earlier. I didn't know yet how it worked.

After I agreed to share some of my allowance, I decided it might be fun if I did it anonymously – and then watched my classmates' reactions. So the next evening I divided my allowance into five dimes, then took two of the dimes and sealed them in small envelopes along with a note signed, "From a Friend."

In the morning I went to class early and slipped the envelopes inside two of the students' desks. Then I sat back and waited for them to arrive. The expressions on their faces as they looked around the classroom were worth the price of my whole allowance. The next week I did it again, this time with three dimes, and the week after that with four.

I remember justifying it by thinking, *Well, now each of us has a dime apiece.* The surprise was how much fun it could be to give to other people.

Fortunately, my grandmother also taught me some business lessons, and showed me the advantages of saving money. But I've never forgotten the looks on the faces of those students – or the lesson it taught me about giving and receiving. This was what I would later come to think of as the Art of Giving.

Finding A Way

Growing up in Gary, I didn't have a lot of friends my own age. I did well in grade school, but was very quiet. I tended to take after my father in that respect more than my mother. In winter, I would be afraid walking to school because of the big kids who'd hurl snowballs at me. I didn't like recess. The kids played a game called Crack the Whip, where a group of children would hold onto one another and form a snake; I'd often be the last one on and get my knees scraped up. So I used to invent excuses to skip recess. One of the excuses was that I loved to paint and draw. It was true, actually, and I was fortunate when my teacher let me work on art projects instead of going out to recess. In a sense, I was never a joiner. But school provided opportunities that fulfilled my love of learning and my growing passion for the arts.

My first ambition was to be a ballet dancer. But I didn't have the physical gifts to be a ballerina (my legs were too short). Then I discovered the comic strip *Brenda Starr*, and decided I wanted to be a newspaper reporter. I loved Brenda's independence and her spunk. When I got to Lew Wallace High School, I signed up to work for the school paper, *The Philosopher*, and soon became the editor. I worked hard, enjoying the gratification of creating something tangible every day, and the paper won a national award during my senior year. That was also where I got my first taste of racial politics. Back then, there was a black high school in downtown Gary that our school wasn't allowed to compete against in sports. I wrote an editorial calling the school's policy undemocratic. As soon as the editorial ran, Verna Hoke, the high school principal, called me in and angrily asked what right I had to criticize the policies of the school. I told her I wasn't criticizing, I was editorializing. "That's what an editor does," I said, and naively cited my First Amendment rights as a journalist. Verna Hoke took the editorship away from me for two weeks, thinking it would teach me a lesson. It did, but it wasn't the lesson she wanted me to learn.

When I was 13, my father began having trouble breathing. He was diagnosed with an enlarged heart and, for the next three years, was in and out of hospitals. He spent much of his time on oxygen. Sophie had her own bungalow by then and my mother thought it would be better for all of us if I went to live with her while she kept my brother, who was then six years old. My mother loved my father very much and was by his side constantly, practically living at the hospital.

Also living at my grandmother's house was my Aunt Ruth ("The Tumor") and her husband. My job became cooking dinner for the four of us each night. This was mostly a matter of survival – Sophie's idea of cooking a roast was to put the meat in four inches of water, pour a lot of paprika on top, then place an onion in the water and let it cook. I used to tell her that anyone who can read can learn to cook. She would say, "Not so." Sophie just didn't have the interest in domestic duties. She always preferred wheeling and dealing. My lifelong love of cooking began in those days of making dinner for my grandmother.

Sophie gave me my sex education, too, which consisted of just one rule: "Never let a boy kiss you on the lips."

Later, when boys would take me out, my grandmother would always turn on the porch light as soon as we returned home to ensure that there was no attempt at hanky panky. The summer after my senior year, grandmother finally found a boy that she approved of – literally the boy next door, who was just home from military school. She thought he was nice, well-mannered and respectable. "He's a lovely boy," she kept telling me. "Maybe you could go to a movie." She pushed this agenda so much that finally I agreed to go out with him, even though he didn't seem so respectable to me.

He picked me up in his convertible, drove straight for the dunes and parked. That wasn't so unusual. Lots of kids did that. But once he began attacking me, the only way I could stop him was by saying, "Whatever you're trying to do, you know your mother's going to hear about it tomorrow." He leaned back, turned the key and drove me home, dropping me off at the curb. And that, as we used to say, was that.

My grandmother was my first important teacher. She steered me onto paths I would follow all of my life, showed me how to get past failures and take creative detours when necessary. She told me "You can do it" when I was certain I couldn't do it, and instilled in me a love of learning. Sophie's own life seemed to reflect something Marie Curie once said: "Nothing in life is to be feared. It is only to be understood."

I remember deciding during my father's funeral that I was going to make my own way through life. My life would be an adventure, and I wasn't going to take a penny from anyone else ever again. I *did* work my way through college, supporting myself with several jobs – but I also accepted the five-dollar bills that Sophie would send me with her letters from home.

Sometimes, I wish that I could sit and talk with Sophie again because I don't think I ever thanked her or told her what a remarkable person she was. After I went away to college, she wrote to me frequently. "My darling Myra," her letters all began.

"I have been thinking about you, knowing that you are doing well and taking care of yourself and not getting into trouble."

She often said that she wanted to come visit, to see where I lived and how college life was treating me. But she never did. She died of pneumonia early in my sophomore year. I have always accepted death as a normal part of being human. But that doesn't mean I didn't miss Sophie. There have been many times over the years when I wished that I could sit and talk with her. Sophie's example and the love and kindness she shared inspired me to want to help others. My grandmother didn't see the obstacles most people saw. I've often wondered why that was. What was it that drove her? I'm not sure. I suppose it was just that she wanted to be someone. If I could say one thing to Sophie, I'd tell her this: "You were." I wish I could tell her that.

TWO

Something from Nothing

"What lies behind us and what lies before us are tiny matters compared to what lies within us." – Ralph Waldo Emerson

"The Possible's slow fuse is lit by the Imagination." – Emily Dickinson

I left home at seventeen, bound for Indiana State University in Terre Haute. Boarding the bus in Gary, I had ten dollars in my purse and my mother's babushka on my head. I felt the nervous excitement that goes with making a new start. The seven-hour bus trip south seemed like a journey to a new life – which it was.

Not knowing anyone in Terre Haute, I understood that I would have to prove myself again. But I felt good about the school and its president, whose name was Ralph Tirey. He wooed me to his university in part because I had been a national debate winner, and Indiana State offered me a full four-year scholarship. He believed in me, and encouraged me, and we remained friends for many years.

When my bus arrived in Terre Haute, President Tirey was there to greet me at the station and take me to lunch. It was a nice welcome. Although I had no place to stay and no source of income, I felt confident – determined to make my own way. In truth, I had little choice. My father's illness had used up the family savings; my mother had begun selling insurance to make ends meet.

But fortune comes more often to those who are ready for it than to those who aren't. It's a truism that worked to my advantage in Terre Haute, where things fell into place quickly. Dr. Tirey introduced me to Dean Charlotte Burford, who knew of a woman on campus – a teacher and writer – with a spare room. I could probably stay with her in exchange for typing her manuscripts.

Typing a writer's manuscripts intrigued me, so I looked up this woman, whose name was Goldie Kinder Hiatt, and she invited me to have supper with her that night. It was quite an experience. I could tell right away that she was a little eccentric and more than a little independent. But I liked her – her wildly varied interests and work ethic reminded me a little of my grandmother.

Goldie lived by herself, with seven or eight cats. She had graying, braided hair and wore what seemed to be a doily around her neck. Her cooking took some getting used to. I'd never had hominy grits before, or homemade biscuits with gravy. Green beans I'd had – but never the way Goldie fixed them. Hers were gray, so overcooked that it felt as if I were chewing on rubber. Somehow, I politely finished Goldie's meal, and we got to know, and like, one another.

"If you want this job, it's yours," she said, finally. "You'll have to do some cleaning, too. I need someone who can really scrub the toilet bowl." I just looked at her when she said that. I hardly knew how to make a bed at the time, but I agreed to do it.

'Try It'

I hadn't been on campus long when I saw a notice on a bulletin board that the editorship of the Indiana State weekly newspaper, *The Statesman*, was open. I still had notions about becoming Brenda Starr so, naturally, this intrigued me. There was just one problem: I was a freshman and the editor was traditionally a senior.

Goldie made a face when I told her this. She made an even stranger face when I insisted. "That's ridiculous," she said. "If you're capable, it doesn't matter if you're a senior or a freshman. Just fill out the application and leave the space blank where they ask for your grade level. Just try it."

I hadn't thought of that. But I did it. The application required an essay describing why we felt qualified to become editor. In a sense, what we were being asked to do was write advertising copy about ourselves. I could do that.

A few days later, the faculty member in charge of journalism called me in. She didn't know me, but she was impressed by my essay. As we talked, she also seemed impressed by my enthusiasm. "Well, I think you're the person for this job," she said. It paid $5 a week. I was elated. It didn't matter that I was a freshman. Goldie had been right.

I still had my work to do for Goldie, of course, which included washing and ironing clothes. I had never done these sorts of chores before but was willing to give it a try. Every Monday, while Goldie was away teaching, I was to do the laundry. My first attempt did not go so well. I quickly got my hand stuck in the ringer of her Maytag washing machine, and had to unplug it. It wasn't pleasant. My hand smarted all day and began to turn black and blue – and I decided that I would never again do laundry. Instead, I took all the clothes, which were soaking wet, out of the washing machine, threw them in a gunny sack and walked down the street to the Chinese laundry. They told me they would wash and press them for $3.50, which I could afford – just barely.

When I picked up the clothes later that day, they were neatly pressed and folded in green wrapping paper. I took off the wrapping paper and burned it in the alley, then neatly stacked the clothes on the shelves in the closet. When Goldie returned home, she was so happy. "I've never had a student who could wash and iron so well," she said. Tears came into my eyes at that point. She thought it was because I was overjoyed at what she had told me. But it was really because I was thinking how I'd have to keep paying $3.50 a week to do our laundry.

It continued for three weeks. One night, a friend of Goldie's named Marguerite Debbs (the niece of labor leader Eugene Debbs) came over to the house and Goldie showed her how I had washed and pressed the laundry. Marguerite said, "Can you do mine, too?" That's when I realized I had to do something to make a little extra money.

But I also felt guilt, getting credit for something I wasn't really doing, and I decided I had to tell Goldie the truth.

"You and I need to talk," I told her.

I remember her sitting there calmly, her silhouette in the window.

"I didn't do it," I said, nervously. "I didn't do the laundry."

She looked at me. "Well, who did?"

So I told her about the Chinese laundry.

To my surprise, she said, "Well, why didn't I think of that? They do such a good job. From now on, we'll use the Chinese laundry."

The reason I hadn't told Goldie the truth at first was because I was afraid she would be disappointed and that I would lose my standing with her. Instead, she turned the situation into a positive lesson and made me feel good. That, as I learned, was the kind of person Goldie was – encouraging, not discouraging.

It was at about this time – when my weekly expenses included the Chinese laundry – that I decided to see if there might be any work available at the city newspaper, the *Terre Haute Star*.

I brazenly walked into the newsroom one day and asked to see the editor. I showed him my clippings and explained that I would accept a position as either a reporter or editor. The editor, Mr. Marcy Cox, scanned my stories for about a minute and then handed them back to me. "I'm sorry," he said. "We're not hiring paper dolls right now. We need experienced reporters who can write." There was a popular song on the radio at the time called "Paper Dolls" ("I'd rather have a paper doll to call my own, Than a fickle-minded real live girl."), and I felt very insulted.

"But I'll tell you what," Mr. Cox added. "We can try you out on obituaries."

"Thank you," I said, "but I don't want to do obituaries."

Walking out of there, I was livid. His comment about the paper dolls caught me completely by surprise. I remember thinking, *I'm going to show those people*. So I looked up the street and saw Meis department store, which was the largest store in Terre Haute at the time. I walked in and asked to speak to the advertising manager – which was how I did things then. His name was Sol Korshack and he seemed amused to see this intense young woman asking for him. We talked for a few minutes and then fortune winked at me. "As a matter of fact," he said, "I'm looking for a copy girl. We can give it a try."

I worked part-time at Meis, writing copy for their advertisements, a job that earned me $7.35 a week. Coupled with my student newspaper salary, it meant I was bringing home $12.35 a week. This seemed like pretty good money to me, although with two jobs I was always running from one place to the other, from Wabash Avenue to the campus and back again.

About six months into the Meis job, Sol Korshack left to join the service. The company president, Salo Levite, asked if I could "keep things together" until he brought in someone from New York to run the department. The Meis advertising department was a small outfit, with a layout person, two copywriters and a manager. They referred to me as "Janco" or "The Kid."

"Sure," I told him. But what I was really thinking was, *Well, now I have a chance to prove myself*. I saw this as an opportunity – not to "keep things together," but to sell myself to Mr. Levite.

For some time I had thought that our ads would be more distinctive if we used our own art work. Now I had a chance to find out if that was true. A shipment of cotton dresses that sold for $7.95 in Junior Miss sizes had just come in to the store. So I worked on my own and designed a double truck ad – "Cool as Lemonade," it read. "Cotton Dresses $7.95." Along with this type, I envisioned an illustration of a girl sitting on the rim of a glass of lemonade, waving a straw. I did the layout and created the illustration. The response when the ad came out was overwhelming. We sold every one of those dresses.

The "Cool as Lemonade" campaign was a pivotal point for me. When Salo Levite saw it, he said, "Who did that? Who decided to do that ad?"

I told him.

"Well, I don't need someone to come in from New York, then. You can do it." Of course, I was still in school at the time, which made things difficult. He wanted me to quit school and work for him full-time. I said, "I can't do that. But I'll come in at six o'clock in the morning, get everything done, then I'll go to my nine o'clock class. Then I'll come back and work here until I have to go to class again at 4:30 and 6:30 and then I'll come back and work here until midnight."

And as crazy as that seemed, it's more or less what I did. As Mr. Levite's assistant, I learned to evaluate the corporate portfolio, went to market with buyers and coordinated all the merchandising and advertising with the buyers. My salary was six thousand five hundred dollars. Within a year, he increased it to ten thousand dollars, which made me the highest paid woman in Terre Haute in those days. And I was just a kid – not even 19.

Mr. Levite had a nephew named Lucien, who came in part-time and worked for me. He lives here in Florida now and not long ago he called me up. "Do you know you started me off in business?" he asked. He had gone on to become president of the chain of department stores, and retired early because he had made so much money.

I trace all that happened to me in Terre Haute to Goldie saying, "Just try it." Yes, it was unprecedented for a freshman to become editor of the university paper – but not impossible. Goldie urged me to "Try it." When I began to whine and express doubts, she said, "You're being ridiculous. Yes, you can." In doing so, she made my fears and apprehensions *seem* ridiculous – and in retrospect, they were. The worst that could have happened was that I would have been turned down. The worst that would have happened if I *hadn't* applied was that I would have missed an opportunity that led, at least indirectly, to the job at Meis and eventually to a career in advertising.

Success is often a mysterious chain reaction, which rarely follows a predictable pattern. But this much is predictable: You won't find it if you don't take a chance, if you don't teach yourself to seize opportunities.

I firmly believe that we become what we think about. If we think of obstacles, and are always second-guessing ourselves, it will show in our work and in our personality. It's like driving with one foot on the brake and one on the accelerator.

I've always gravitated to "You can do it" people – encouraging souls who seem to believe in me more than I believe in myself. People who know things I don't know, who have talents and experiences I don't have. Goldie turned out to be one of them. She loved teaching young people – it invigorated her – and I became one of her pupils. Before long, I was calling her Aunt Goldie. We also became friends, and stayed friends for thirty-eight years.

The world of advertising seemed tailor-made for me, combining a number of my interests – writing, research, art, business and salesmanship. Not all of my ideas at Meis were as successful as the cotton dresses. One that didn't go over so well was my campaign for navy blue and white polka dot dresses with gumdrop color accessories – lemon lime, strawberry, orange. My idea was to create a window display with big gumdrops. But the gumdrops melted in the sun and it was a disaster. When Salo Levite saw how upset I was, he said, "Janco, we all make mistakes."

Truth in Advertising

I worked at Meis for six years, and then decided I was ready to start my own ad agency. What inspired this bold – some might say foolish – decision? I used to study the ads in magazines such as *Fortune* and I would sometimes think, *I could do that. I could tell the same story, but do it better.* I had no problem selling myself on that notion – I just needed to sell others.

SECRET THREE
Surround Yourself with Teachers

Experience may be a great teacher, but your experiences will be vastly more valuable, and fulfilling, when you associate with people who can instruct, inspire and encourage you, both directly and by example.

Try to associate with people who know things you don't know; who have skills you don't have; who have done things you haven't done; who have been places you haven't been. This will save you time and effort and enable you to avoid many of the pitfalls that you might otherwise encounter. Surround yourself with people who know less than you do, and you may feel smart and talented; but you're not – you're just comfortable, in a rut.

I still seek out people who know things I don't know. As I've gotten older I've come to appreciate more and more how important this is, in fact. My "teachers" keep life stimulating, and an adventure.

There is truth in the old Chinese proverb: "A single conversation with a wise man is better than ten years of study."

Starting my second business was a little more complicated than the first – Janco Party Favors – which I had launched at age four. I had never been in the ad agency business, and knew that it would be difficult to sell a new company to prospective advertisers. The challenge of that excited me but also made me nervous.

It began as a two-person agency, with me as the president, marketing director, research director, copywriter and janitor. At first, I worked from home, then received a loan and was able to rent an office. I called the business Wabash Advertising because it was near the banks of the Wabash River in Terre Haute, Indiana.

Launching Wabash Advertising meant a lot of homework and long hours. It was a learning experience but it was fun because it was a new adventure. I started out by writing letters to prospective clients, and followed them up with phone calls. Sometimes, this would lead to a meeting. My strategy in meeting with business owners was to encourage them to talk about their problems. Then I asked them to let me suggest a solution. My credo was to search out the truth – to get the facts and help them solve their problems.

Wabash Advertising was built on hard work, research and the notion that we could do things other agencies couldn't. We told prospective clients that it wasn't the size of the agency that mattered, it was the size of your ideas; Wabash could offer more individualized attention than the larger agencies in Chicago and St. Louis, we said. Believing this led me to approach several big local accounts – and even some national ones. I studied the *Wall Street Journal*. I looked up companies' Dun & Bradstreet ratings.

I read the glossy business magazines, asking myself, *What is this ad saying? What isn't it saying? Would I respond to this ad?*

One advertiser I discovered in the pages of *Fortune* was the Bledsoe coal company, which ran double-truck, full-color spreads every few months. Knowing the price of those pages, I figured that if I could land just one account of that size, it would more than pay the rent on our limestone office building on Ohio Boulevard. So I went to work learning the coal business.

At the time, Bledsoe was one of the world's largest strip mine operators. Their agency, I discovered, was based in Chicago. We were in Terre Haute, closer to the mines. I also learned that the Bledsoe family was originally from Terre Haute.

When I felt well-versed in coal, I called up the man who ran the company, a Mr. W.S. Webster, to ask for an appointment. It wasn't easy. His assistant, Miss Shirley Pine, did everything she could to keep me from getting through to him. But after much persistence, I got through and scheduled a meeting.

I bought a smart, navy blue dress for the occasion, and a white beret. I went in to the meeting nervous but confident – with lots of research data. I had read that industrial coal sales were falling, and I explained to Mr. Webster how I could help him reach markets he wasn't reaching. I'd also help him come up with a stronger message. My premise was essentially a question: "Are you really doing as much business as you'd like to be doing?" I assured him that I would help him take business away from some of his competitors with a carefully tailored ad campaign, and also help improve his image in the industry. "Just give me three weeks," I said. Mr. Webster seemed a little skeptical, and maybe a little amused, but took me up on my offer: Yes, he would give me three weeks.

The first thing Goldie said to me when I returned home that afternoon was, "Myra! You're not wearing a slip!"

I looked down and saw that she was right. I had bought this new dress, which I thought looked very businesslike, but it was sheer navy blue and I had been so nervous that morning that I must have forgotten to put on a slip. Whether that had anything to do with Mr. Webster's reception, I'll never know. But I didn't worry about it. I had a challenge to sell myself to him, and three weeks to prepare.

In those days, the coal mines all had names. One was called Blue Rose, for instance. Another was Black Beauty. There was a sameness to the coal ads, which all showed pretty pictures. They were competing with one another based on memorable images, but they weren't actually talking about their product. I thought it would be more effective – and unusual – to talk facts.

So I set out to learn everything I could about the business. I talked with miners, I talked with purchasing agents, I talked with competitors, customers and potential customers. I began to develop a creative rationale for a campaign that could increase Bledsoe's business. Several times I was reminded of my father's question when I was preparing to start up Janco Party Favors: Why would anyone want to buy that? I had to give Mr. Webster something that he needed.

During those three weeks, I created a comparative profile of the Bledsoe coal company, which showed that the company wasn't as well-known in key markets as management believed.

When I went back to Mr. Webster's office, I told him things he'd never heard before. I presented the profile of Bledsoe and evaluated the effectiveness of the existing advertising. Bledsoe needed a stronger voice, I urged, and suggested a coordinated campaign of magazine, trade journal and direct mail advertising. I also proposed a fact-based approach that would make Bledsoe's ads stand out.

The ads presented coal buyers with facts that would lead them to purchase Bledsoe "quality" coal. They compared coals and BTU's, mine locations and productivity. The ads will use straight talk, I told Mr. Webster. He smiled. We got Bledsoe away from the Chicago agency. It was our first major account.

Leaving a Bad Taste

While paging through my *Wall Street Journal* one day, I became intrigued by an article about a man named George Appel, who had just retired from Old Mr. Boston, the liquor distillery. I decided right then to call him and ask if he'd be interested in consulting with a small but growing agency in Terre Haute. One of the lessons I learned from Goldie was that young and old people should work together – that each has something to gain from the other. One of the reasons Wabash Advertising was successful was because I brought in retired people as part-time consultants who could tell me what I was doing wrong.

At first, Mr. Appel didn't comment. So I went on the sell, telling him some of the things our little two-person agency had already accomplished. But I still couldn't tell if he was interested.

"Mr. Appel," I said, "how about if I send a plane after you?" I had earned my pilot's license by this time and decided to fly out on my Tri-Pacer to personally bring him to Terre Haute. Hearing this must have convinced him of my earnestness because he accepted.

I had never tasted whiskey at this point but I knew there was a substantial market for whiskey advertising. My thinking was, *If we could get a whiskey ad, we'd have it made*. Because I knew nothing about whiskey, it seemed logical to hire an authority, who could teach me a little about the business and perhaps help me land one of these lucrative accounts.

This was one of the ways I built the agency: By affiliating with people who knew things I didn't know. It's a great way to climb ladders in business and in life – although sometimes it works better than others.

Mr. Appel came into the office three mornings a week to meet with me, and talk whiskey. When he arrived, my assistant, Joyce, would always say, "Your whiskey teacher's here."

Pretty soon, I knew just about everything there was to know about whiskey from a marketing standpoint – and also how it was made. One day Mr. Appel told me about a new product coming on the market, which was based in Chicago; he said he'd like to help us land the account. He went to Chicago to lay the groundwork and then he called me. "They want to meet you," he said. So I put on my beret, fired up my Tri-Pacer and flew up there.

It was mid-morning when I arrived and I hadn't eaten breakfast. Mr. Appel was there already with the chairman of the company. I walked into the chairman's office – a beautiful office with the largest kidney shaped desk I had ever seen – and took a seat.

We talked for a little while and then the chairman looked at me and said, "You really seem to know the whiskey market."

"Thank you."

"Do you know our product? Have you tasted the product?"

"No, sir," I said.

They had little Drambuie glasses lined up on this magnificent desk, I noticed – marked A, B, C, D – along with what I thought was a pot for a plant but turned out to be a spittoon for the whiskey. And I suddenly realized that these men expected me to taste their products that morning.

I thought, *Well, these are very small glasses, I guess I can do it*. After all, this was what I'd been working toward. So I convinced myself to go ahead and sample their whiskey. I drank down the first one and it was just terrible. It burned my throat and tasted something awful. *This is a product I need to sell*, I reminded myself. I quickly put down A and went to B. B was even worse – the vilest taste I'd ever known.

I thought, *We could* never *sell this even if we did the best advertising in the world. Who would buy it?*

But I kept quiet. I went to C, suddenly feeling a little hot. I drank C and pretended to smile and then I lifted D. After drinking that, I sat down, my beret fell off and I went to sleep. When I woke up, I heard voices in the background, laughing. We didn't get the account and I never again went after a whiskey product.

The lesson I learned from the whiskey experience was that I should not try to sell a product – or an idea – that I did not believe in. That became part of my philosophy of advertising. It's a good life lesson, too. Don't try to sell something if you don't understand it or if you don't believe in it.

New Ideas

I learned a sweeter lesson when I went after the Heath candy company account. In those days, Heath not only made candy bars but they also operated a dairy and a soft drink line. They didn't advertise and didn't need to. My encounter with Heath was really a happy accident. I was driving through the Illinois countryside one afternoon when I passed a block-long L.S. Heath and Sons factory. I was on my way back to Terre Haute from visiting another client, but decided I'd stop and have a look. I wasn't sure at first if this was the company headquarters or not, but there was an old man in coveralls out front straightening concrete, so I said to him, "Excuse me, sir. Does Mr. L.S. Heath have offices here?"

"Yep," he said.

And I said, "Is there any chance that I could go in and meet him without an appointment?"

"Yep. I think you could," he said.

I followed him through the offices, which seemed to go on forever. We came at last to a corner office where the man sat down behind this big desk and he said, "Okay. Now what can I do for you?"

I told Mr. Heath a little about my advertising agency. Heath was a big business, and I knew they didn't advertise. "Wait a minute," Mr. Heath said, when I finished talking. "Petey," he called out, "get in here. There's a girl I want you to meet. Vernon, come on in here, I want you to meet this girl. Bayard, there's a girl who wants to meet you." Petey was in charge of soft drinks, it turned out. Vernon was in charge of the dairy and Bayard was in charge of the candy bars. These were men in their fifties and sixties – L.S. Heath's sons.

The three "boys" gathered in the room and Mr. Heath said to them, "She says she's starting an ad agency."

"No, I've already started it."

"Maybe we could show her around the plant," Mr. Heath said.

We went to the dairy first and Mr. Heath cut what must have been a half gallon of Tutti Frutti with his knife, and handed it to me. "Here, Miss Janco, you go ahead and eat this ice cream." I couldn't really eat that much ice cream but I did (and burped Tutti Frutti all the way home).

And then we toured the soft drink business. By the end of that afternoon, I had bonded with these men and felt like we were old friends. Later, when I ran a

Find What You Love – And Do It!

If you aren't in love with what you do, then you haven't found your true calling – and need to make a change. Don't settle for something you don't love. Keep searching.

Some people say they don't know what they want in life. Find out. Ask yourself: *What is it that really makes me happy? What gets me excited?* The answers will steer you to what you should be doing.

You won't reach your true potential – for happiness or success – until you've discovered this calling. The process can take time, requiring trial and error, but it's well worth pursuing. As a teacher and as a business executive, I have often seen how people suddenly blossom when they find work that is ideally suited to them.

national ad agency in Chicago, the "boys" would sometimes stop by our offices on the 25th and 27th floors of the John Hancock Building to say hello.

But on that afternoon, I had a dilemma: How could I interest these men in advertising? I remembered my father's question again, and began to think about it. I had to tell them something they needed, something they didn't know or hadn't been told before.

But what? As I stood there watching the candy bars come off the line, I noticed that there were are all these leftover crumbs.

"What do you do with all those toffee and chocolate crumbs?" I asked.

Mr. Heath said, "Oh, we give them to our friends. They like to put them on ice cream and desserts. Would you like a bag?"

It occurred to me at that point that they had three products that could be combined to create a new product – ice cream and toffee and chocolate. Why not put them together? That was one of my ideas that helped me win their business. The toffee-and-chocolate-ice-cream-bar later became a popular product. I also showed them an advertisement in the form of a newspaper column, which included recipes for desserts that could be made with Heath products. No one had done that before. I created a book with fifty recipes using Heath products, which we sold through the mail for twenty-five cents.

It worked. How was I able to sell myself to a client who didn't need to advertise? By showing them that they *did* need to advertise. In this case, just being green, having enthusiasm and wanting to try new things won the day. Confidence, I have long thought, is a close cousin of fear. We act confidently because we don't want to fail, and the more we succeed, the more the two become more distant relatives. As Eleanor Roosevelt once said, "You gain strength, courage and confidence by every experience in which you really stop to look fear in the face . . . You must do the thing you cannot do."

I try to do the thing I cannot do, and often surprise myself. That's how Wabash Advertising grew. By the end of our first year, we had ten full-time employees and a million dollars worth of business.

Learn to Take Intelligent Risks

One of the least understood – but most important – elements of success, in virtually every field, is the ability to take intelligent risks. I've known many talented people over the years who were never able to master the art of intelligent risk-taking and, consequently, often came up short – in business and in life.

When it comes to what I call "risk intelligence," people seem to fall into one of two categories: They either maintain an aversion to risk-taking or else they take occasional risks that in retrospect seem careless, without being properly prepared, or fully understanding the consequences. Each year, for instance, some six hundred thousand people start up their own businesses in the United States. The statistics about these risk-takers are pretty grim: Less than five percent of these businesses survive five years. More than half fail in the first year.

Most people associate the concept of "risk" with failure. "It seems risky" is another way of saying "Don't do it." The term "intelligent risk," in this sense, becomes something of an oxymoron. But if we spend just a few minutes examining and questioning our assumptions about risk, we can turn this stereotype upside down – and maybe change our lives.

Think of risk as a stepping stone on the path to what you really want in your life. For virtually all of the successful people I know, and have known, this is exactly what it is.

These are what I call the five steps of intelligent risk-taking:

1. An intelligent risk is, first and foremost, something you feel passionate about. The first step in intelligent risk-taking is gauging your desire. Another way of looking at this is "The How versus Why Test." When people contemplate risk-taking, they often

wonder, "How am I going to do this?" That's the wrong question. The more important question is, "Why am I going to do this?" If the answer is because you passionately want to do it, then you should proceed. If the answer is you're not sure, or if you're doing it because you're unhappy in your job, say, or because you want to make a lot of money, then you shouldn't.

Be honest and take a sober look at yourself when you pose this question. If you're wrestling with the answer, then you don't want it enough and the risk is not worth taking.

2. Do your homework. Too many people pass the first test, then don't prepare properly. This is one of the main reasons that risk turns to failure. If your intelligent risk involves starting a business, learn everything you can about the field. Know your market and know your competitors. Ask yourself, "What gaps are there in the marketplace and how can I fill them?" Sometimes, this second phase will turn up compelling evidence that the risk you are contemplating is not a good one. That's fine. Feeling passionate isn't, alone, enough to justify taking an intelligent risk. Make sure your passion to take the risk is supported by facts. Don't go into the "gamble" of intelligent risk-taking until you have a clear understanding of the odds.

3. Write out a "creative rationale." I'm convinced this is a key part of turning risks to rewards. Formulate a strategy, write it out, and review it (and rewrite it, when necessary) rather than just keep it in your head. The creative rationale should examine how your plan will make you stand out from others. This should be more than a financial plan – that comes in Step 2. It should be a philosophy and a strategy.

4. Have a sounding board or two (but not many more than that). One of the main reasons that people take unintelligent risks and fail is that they listen to the wrong people. When I look at the risks I've taken that weren't intelligent, it was usually because I let myself be talked into the risk-taking and didn't spend enough time on Steps 2 and 3.

Sometimes we fail because we gather too many opinions – from people who reinforce our desire to take a risk, but who haven't thoroughly weighed the pros and cons.

Learn to listen to yourself – and to trust yourself. But also have one or two people you trust who can help you see your plan in a fresh light. If they respond with enthusiasm, you are ready to move to Step 5. If not, you need to do some more homework.

5. Transform your creative rationale into action – but be prepared to adapt and improvise. Some people do so much homework and plan their strategy so precisely that they don't know what to do when unexpected obstacles turn up. Part of intelligent risk-taking requires improvising or taking "creative detours." It's important to "expect" unexpected obstacles.

THREE

Life's Classroom

"It has always seemed strange to me that in our endless discussions about education so little stress is laid on the pleasure of becoming an educated person, the enormous interest it adds to life. To be able to be caught up into the world of thought – that is to be educated." – Edith Hamilton

"I have never let my schooling interfere with my education." – Mark Twain

Knowing what "matters" in life – in business, relationships, spirituality – can save us a great deal of wasted time and effort. But it's a tricky subject, because what matters changes as we get older – and as we discover that so many of those things we once thought were important really aren't.

I think I was twenty-five when I first began to recognize that success was not as big a deal as I had thought. Or, maybe, I began to think that success, for me, needed to be redefined. I owned an advertising agency that was generating a million dollars worth of business. If I was a success, though, I sure didn't feel like one. Something was missing in my life. Success in itself wasn't the result I was seeking. I wanted something more. I had to do some thinking and get through some restless days.

Many of the goals that we strive for most fervently, particularly in our youth, turn out to be worth much less than we imagined once we attain them and try to "cash them in." When I was in my mid-twenties, I began to understand that results were less important than staying challenged. Security, which we all strive for, is not the same as satisfaction; pleasure is not the same as happiness. The line between being comfortable and becoming complacent is often not a line at all – it is an invisible no man's land that can steal away our potential if we linger there too long. The best goal, I decided – the real measure of success – was to always keep life challenging.

As Leonardo da Vinci wrote in his *Notebooks*, "Experience never errs. It is only your judgments that err by promising results which are not caused by your experiments." What I needed were better, more rewarding experiments.

The success of Wabash Advertising was based on a strategy of supplying clients with information that they did not know about themselves, and giving them new means of solving problems. To continue growing, I needed to find more sophisticated ways of doing this. Put more simply, I began to realize that I didn't know enough. *If I can do this well without knowing anything*, I thought, *what could I do if I really knew research?*

My solution was to go back to school – both figuratively and literally. I enrolled in a doctorate program in marketing management at Indiana University, which, at the time, had one of the top business schools in the country. It didn't mean closing my agency, but it meant turning my focus from it for a while.

There was one other factor that contributed to my return to school: I was engaged to be married and when the engagement broke off, I decided I needed a change in my life.

SECRET SIX
Go Back to School

One of the essential qualities of "rutbusting" is being able to wake yourself up when you've fallen asleep.

No matter how successful we are, we must continually evaluate who and where we are and what we're doing. Successful people never stop "going back to school." They develop the instinct of knowing when they are becoming stale, when it's time to make a change, when they need to learn fresh lessons – whether in their jobs or their personal lives.

Contrary to what people are taught to think, we can change who we are at any point in our lives – we can move into careers better suited for our skills; we can lose bad habits and gain good ones. I have seen this so many times that it makes me sad when I hear people say, "Oh, I could never do that" or "But I'm too old." Often a minor adjustment in our habits or thinking can result in a major change in our lives. But we first have to recognize that we need to make this adjustment – to "go back to school."

I have met so many people over the years who only needed a small push – a word of encouragement, a promotion, a loan, a piece of advice – and they might have found their path to contentment and success. Too often that small push never came.

The way I determine when I need to go back to school is by regularly taking inventory – taking a disgustingly honest look at myself.

The most significant lesson I learned by going to graduate school was how much I didn't know. It was a sobering but ultimately invigorating lesson. Having to dissect the complexities of successful marketing and management forced me to think more deeply, and intelligently, about things I had begun to take for granted. It was a good exercise. Although I was enrolled in a doctoral marketing program, what I was really studying was, in a sense, myself.

Returning to school seemed to nurture a seed that my grandmother had planted years earlier – the idea that learning should be a continuing, lifelong adventure, not just something we do to pass tests or hang diplomas on our walls. Going back to school opened me up to a larger world beyond that defined by my job. It took down the walls that I looked at every day and let me explore a rich realm of ideas, history and possibilities.

I kept my agency, which I moved to Chicago, but devoted most of my time to the doctoral program. I bought a house in Bloomington, Indiana, right off campus, and "Aunt Goldie," as I called her, came to live with me. By this time, she did, indeed, seem like a family member. Goldie enrolled in a creative writing class and began to write for pay. Her sewing skills also made her one of the costume mistresses for a nearby opera school.

My philosophy about education then was to think of the university as a laboratory for learning. I always preferred real-world, hands-on education to theoretical textbook learning. This became my creed as a teacher. It still is. At our arts center in Florida, we offer more than a hundred and fifty adult education classes each year, taught by scholars and experts in their fields. But they're more than just classes; many are intimate, interactive sessions that give participants the rare opportunity to partner with nationally known visual and performing artists. If the sessions aren't fun or enlightening, there's no point in continuing them.

Giving Shelter

One of my favorite teachers at Indiana University was a man named Dorcey Forrest. Dorcey had a lively passion for learning and I enjoyed talking with him about marketing and the advertising business. Because of my advertising experience, Dorcey would sometimes let me teach his class when he was out of town. I never expected, though, that when he resigned to become head of the advertising department at New York University, he would go to the dean and recommend that I take over for him.

I remember how I heard the news. The night before, all the doctoral candidates had been over to my house for dinner. I served them shepherd's pie, with about seven different meats and ten different vegetables. In those days, there were no women in this doctoral program at Indiana University; I was also the only doctoral candidate who owned a house and the only one who could cook. So, occasionally, I would invite the guys over to my house to test out a new recipe; then we'd settle down and study together.

In the course of that evening, the guys teased me a little bit, as they customarily did. One of them said, "Myra, you should call Art Weimer. I understand he's free again." Weimer was dean of the business school at the time – a tough, brilliant man who had been married something like four or five times.

Early the next morning, I received a call.

"Miss Janco?" a male voice said.

"Yes?"

He said, "This is Art Weimer. I'd like you to come over to my office."

"Oh?" I said. "I know what *you* want."

"Excuse me?"

"Who is this, really?" I asked, assuming it was one of the guys playing a joke.

He said, "Miss Janco, this IS Arthur Weimer and I DO want to see you."

"Oh?" As I walked across campus to his office, I became a little worried, wondering if somehow I'd flunked out. Dean Weimer was waiting for me behind his desk, looking over the top of his glasses, appearing very somber. He nodded for me to have a seat and he took a breath.

"Miss Janco," he said, "Dorcey Forrest has resigned. He thinks you would be a good person to fill his boots."

"Oh," I said. "But I couldn't do that."

"Why not?"

"Well. For one thing, I still have my ad agency in Chicago and I fly a plane back and forth."

He said, "We'll make allowances for that if you'll help us out." And then he added, "I can make you an associate professor."

"Oh?" *An associate professor*! I thought. That was one rank below full professor, unheard of for someone who doesn't have a doctorate degree yet. Also, no woman had ever held that position in the business school. I told him yes, and then more or less floated back home. There was a river on campus, the Jordan River, that I used to cross and I think on that morning I may have actually walked on water.

I knew the job would be good for my resume, even though I'd only be doing it for the remainder of that semester. Or so I thought. As it turned out, I wound up holding a six-year associate professorship in marketing and advertising at Indiana University, directing an internship program in publishing.

Once I became a teacher, my greatest responsibility, I felt, was to make education interesting – but also relevant. One of the messages I tried to get across to my students was this: Make life your classroom, not this little room where we meet three times a week. Too much of institutionalized education is theoretical and textbook-oriented. I wanted to teach them to think beyond the classroom.

One of the ways I did this was by helping to start up a magazine called *Business Horizons*. It was funded by a Ford Foundation grant, which supplied me with the budget to hire a staff of twenty students, who operated an internal advertising agency and the sales department for the magazine. The students were paid fifty dollars a week plus expenses.

Business Horizons was sort of a poor man's *Harvard Business Review*. We covered national business stories, profiled CEOs and analyzed management and leadership trends. The magazine gave us an excuse to travel, to gain first-hand knowledge about the workings of corporate America, while selling advertising space in the magazine and researching stories. To our surprise, some of the most established CEOs agreed to be interviewed. It was a lot of work, yes, but most of the time we were having so much fun we didn't notice. At the end of the first quarter, our interns not only paid their own expenses and salaries, but they had brought in thousands of dollars in ad revenue. Some of the participants in that class went on to become company presidents and CEOs, television, radio and newspaper executives.

Another way of reaching beyond the walls of the classroom was to bring seasoned business leaders to talk with students and answer their questions. Seeing them in a classroom setting made their achievements more tangible than simply reading about them. Sometimes, I would present the class with real-life problems I'd read about in the *Wall Street Journal* or *Business Week* and ask them to devise hypothetical solutions.

Among the most memorable real-world exercises was one we tackled in a Public Relations class. More than 100,000 stray animals lived in Monroe County at the time, but the county had no rabies clinic and no shelter for strays. There were more strays in Monroe County than in any other county in the state, and the Monroe County Humane Society was increasingly under pressure to solve the problem. If you were the president of the Humane Society, what would you do? That was the exercise.

The class split up into groups of five and devised some creative, cogent ideas. The best solution was to raise money for a shelter, we decided, but how could it be done? We determined that a shelter and rabies clinic would cost about $10,000 to build. Then I said to the class, "Okay, let's do it. We've got three days."

There were some raised eyebrows when I said that. "Is this for real?" some of them asked.

"Sure," I said. "Why not?"

Turning a hypothetical into a real-life challenge motivated the students. So did my faith that they could do it. It also motivated me, and I became the baton twirler for the project. My students left the classroom and went out into the world to implement their plans. First, they notified the newspapers and radio stations about what they were doing. Then they prepared a press release and called a press conference. They also networked with the student body, the fraternities and sororities, generating word of mouth interest in their campaign all over campus.

They attached baskets to the necks of German Shepherd dogs from the fraternities and walked them around the town square, collecting money. People gave. The excitement of the cause became contagious. On Saturday night, the students gathered at my house and counted up the money. In three days, they had collected just over nine thousand dollars. Goldie counted it out. I wrote out a check for the rest, and the shelter was built.

The lesson that we all learned from this exercise was that people *can* do almost anything when they're galvanized and they share belief. I'm sometimes asked how I manage to motivate people, how I'm able to get them excited about a project. It's simple: By being excited myself.

The Politics of Education

Despite many rewarding experiences at Indiana University, my tenure there was, in the end, bittersweet. One of the tough lessons I learned was that the halls of ivy aren't always pure. I'd been there six years when I discovered a problem with the funding of our business magazine. Examining the books, I realized that profits were being funneled away from the magazine; it turned out that a faculty member was taking kickbacks from the project.

People deal with dishonesty differently. Some become outraged and confrontational; others look the other way. I'm not real good at confrontation (although I've gotten better). What particularly irked me in this case was that my students had worked so hard to make this magazine a success. I couldn't look the other way because I was the one who submitted the financial reports to the Ford Foundation. So I went to the dean and told him what was happening, expecting him to confront the man. But he surprised me; he told me he couldn't do that. The man in question was a full professor, with tenure. The dean explained that it would be too much trouble and cause too much disgrace to make a public fuss.

The dean's attitude threw me. I loved teaching, and working with my students. The university had become for me a laboratory for learning, yielding deeper insights and more fulfilling rewards than I was getting from the advertising business. But I knew I couldn't work under those conditions. I also didn't think I could win if I tried to fight the dean. So I went in and resigned, effective at the end of the semester. The news came out in the student daily the next day; they made up a quote from me saying that my job was stressful with all the other work I was doing for my agency. Both the dean and the chancellor made flattering comments.

Not many people would walk away from the job I had. But something bothered me very deeply by this point. It was a time of disillusionment in my life, when I realized I had been naïve and probably too optimistic in my expectations. It went beyond the faculty member taking kickbacks. It was the mindset of institutionalized learning, which had allowed it to occur. Of course, there are many honorable, effective and brilliant people in academia, who serve the calling well. But there are a handful of others who fall asleep once they are tenured, and some who take advantage in other ways. Institutionalized education allows them to do so. I was disillusioned by the way the wheels of academia seemed to grind so slowly, and by how people could snore loudly and never get caught.

Although I left the world of education in 1961, I never really did. I still push myself both as a student and as a teacher. My heart still belongs to teaching. In fact, teaching is what I am still doing. Not preacher-teaching, but guiding people toward the truths in their lives. Gently helping them to wake up when they've fallen asleep or become slaves to their habits. I try to do the same with myself, taking inventory every six months, asking which habits in my life have become negative, reminding myself, *If today isn't exciting, then something's wrong; I need to change something in my life*. Usually, it means that habits have gotten in the way of curiosity.

By this time, my advertising agency, based in Chicago, was doing well and I knew I could return full-time to the world of advertising. Making the decision to leave the university was difficult, however. While struggling with it, I shared my thoughts with a man named Ernie Butler, a handyman working at my home. Ernie was also a minister, who led an African American congregation in a poor section of town. With eight children to support, he earned extra income by washing cars, mowing lawns and doing fix-up work. Reverend Butler was a man of deep faith and a lot of common sense – more than I had. As I told him the problem I was wrestling with, he listened patiently. Afterward, he told me, matter-of-factly, what I should do. "Saying no to one thing is a way of saying yes to something else," he added.

It was good advice. I said no to the university, and returned to advertising. But I never left the larger classroom I had learned to love during my years in academia. I still go there each day.

SECRET SEVEN
Redefine Failure

Failure has one great advantage over success: The potential to teach us important lessons. Too many people try to "get past" failures, "to put it behind" them, rather than to figure out what went wrong and why. Without this understanding, they often end up repeating the same mistakes. In this way, failure can become a habit.

One of the salient differences between people who are content and successful is how they handle failure.

Failure, like success, is simply a word we need to redefine. If success means being able to spend life in your own way, failure is an obstacle to that goal. Anticipate failure and look for ways around it. As Thomas Edison said: "Many of life's failures are people who did not realize how close they were to success when they gave up."

Don't make room for failure in your life, in other words, but understand that it is inevitable. Use it. Accept it. Become wiser because of it. Always learn from failure. Don't run from it or deny it. Redefine it – not as a calamity but as a necessity. **Success is often a liar. Failure is what keeps us honest.**

FOUR

Rutbusting

"The chief enemy of creativity is 'good' sense'." – Pablo Picasso

"The unfortunate thing about this world is that the good habits are much easier to give up than the bad ones." – W. Somerset Maugham

Returning to advertising, I moved to Evanston, just outside of Chicago, where I bought a house on Michigan Avenue – a much-too-large, white colonial with twelve rooms, where I lived with Aunt Goldie, a white collie dog we named Yoo Hoo Dammit and four cats.

I chose Evanston because I thought I might join the faculty at Northwestern University. But as soon as I got a taste for the advertising business again, I knew I'd never go back to formal teaching. This was an exciting time in advertising, a time of bold, colorful, creative campaigns that seemed to be transforming advertising into a new American art form.

One of my accounts in those days was with the American Trucking Association. They came to us not to advertise a product but to solve a problem: how to swing business going to privately-owned trucking fleets back to common carriers. The tonnage of the former had increased more than fivefold in recent years over that of the common carriers. I threw myself into researching the issue – as I had done years earlier with coal and whiskey – learning all that I could about the trucking business. I talked to truckers, I talked to their customers. The only thing that kept me from actually driving a truck was that my legs were too short.

The campaign that I eventually created for the ATA was based on "straight talk" (before John McCain began using the term). It detailed the advantages of regulated highway common carriers over the high costs of "do it yourself" trucking. The campaign worked, causing more than a thousand companies to switch from private truckers to common carriers. I became the first woman invited to be a member of the Sales Council of the ATA.

For three years in a row – in 1961, 1962 and 1963 – the agency managed to win national advertising awards. In 1963, a new advertising agency, Roche, Rickard, Henri, Hurst Inc., was formed by a merger of Chicago's two oldest ad firms and I was chosen for the position of executive vice president, the first female vice president for either of these firms. My academic background, combined with my business management and market research experience, won me the job, I was told.

As executive vice president, my role was more management than creative. This was a distinguished company, located on Michigan Avenue, which had been in business for fifty-two years. It was run by well-heeled Ivy League men who walked around with fobs and three-piece suits and belonged to the best clubs in town. But the agency had recently lost its biggest account – Studebaker-Packard – and needed some fresh ideas. One of my first tasks was to trim staff and reshuffle personnel. It took about three months before I felt we were operating efficiently.

What we really needed, though, was a first-rate creative genius. Without one, we would never be competitive with the top agencies. I told this to the chairman,

James Probstein, one day. He was sitting at his desk reading the farm journal, which was what most interested him – farming equipment and farming. He looked up at me and nodded, but I didn't think he really wanted to change. Again, it seemed that I had run up against people who were set in their ways, who had gone to sleep. But Mr. Probstein was not asleep and, it turned out, he was willing to listen.

Rutbuster

In 1965, a couple of things happened that changed my life. Both were unexpected. One was winning the national Advertising Woman of the Year honor. Awards never meant a lot to me. Even today, I don't put them on my walls. I'm more interested in what I'm building than in what I've built.

But receiving this award was a nice surprise. Usually, it went to more seasoned advertising executives from New York. I was the youngest woman who had ever won it – the first woman under forty. Also, I had not applied for it, and had no idea that anyone had nominated me. I didn't realize I'd won until I was looking through some telegrams I brought home from the office and noticed the one from the American Advertising Federation. Finally, I understood why people had been smiling and congratulating me all afternoon.

Some five thousand people gathered in Philadelphia for the award ceremony. It was a big deal, but it didn't change me much. It did change how some people acted toward me, though. After that honor, I received invitations to speak all over the country. I had inquiries about writing a book. Much was made of the fact that I was a female executive in a man's world. "The only woman in the boardroom," I was called.

It's true that advertising was still a man's club back in the 1960s, at least at the executive level. But I never thought in terms of gender and don't recall running into any problems being a woman. Sometimes, it worked to my advantage. But I didn't think much about it. That wasn't what mattered. What mattered was: *How do you increase your sales and improve your image?* Also, I didn't think of what I did as a solo effort. I've always succeeded by partnering with others, by sharing the excitement of working toward a mutual goal.

Others, though, did think about it. Articles about me all pointed out that I was a female executive "in the male-dominated advertising world." More than once, I was asked if there was ever any resentment over the fact that I was a young woman running a national firm. My response was, "If so, I must not have been smart enough to notice." I tried to block out things like that.

I always thought of myself as an ad person, not an ad woman. What differentiated me more than my gender, I thought, was my academic background and my interest in research. What made me succeed were ideas that had nothing to do with gender – selling "benefits" to the customer, searching out the truth, identifying problems and generating creative solutions.

One of those who interviewed me after I was named Advertising Woman of the Year was Auren Uris, the bestselling author of several business books. Uris was at work on a book called *The Executive Breakthrough*, which dissected the character traits and management philosophies of several American business leaders. He wanted to include a chapter on me, which he wound up calling "President in A Gray Flannel Skirt."

"The least likely type that Myra Janco might be compared to is the Western gambler," he wrote. "Yet again and again in her career, she demonstrated the fact that she was not reluctant to take risks. In her own words, she sought out 'the adventure of being different.'" Uris called this trait "Rut Busting."

I had been called many names before, but never a rutbuster – and I wasn't sure at first that I liked the sound of it. These days, I like the word. I think it says a lot about what I believe. The main reason most people fail to achieve what they want in life is that they become stuck – bound to habits or doubts or the expectations of others.

When I look at some of the people I admire, I see "rutbusters" – men and women who have taken creative detours to forge their own uniquely successful paths through life.

People such as my friend Edward Villella, for many years the leading male ballet dancer in this country. Edward was a trailblazer, who took dance into new aesthetic and creative territory. His work with George Balanchine and the New York City Ballet in the 1950s and '60s was legendary. Then a tragic thing happened to Edward. He was dancing at the White House for President and Mrs. Ford in 1974 when his hip socket gave out, ending his dancing career.

For a man who loved his work as Edward did, learning that he would never be able to dance again was difficult, to say the least. He might have retired, and spent the rest of his life giving talks, consulting, writing books – or just traveling and "enjoying life." But Edward was not made that way; he wouldn't have been happy in retirement.

In the mid-1980s, Edward began recruiting some of the finest dancers, designers and choreographers in the country to form a new ballet company. Today, the Miami City Ballet is regarded as one of the world's virtuoso dance troupes – and as its founder and artistic director, Edward is involved in all aspects of the operation.

I think, too, of Muriel Siebert, who dropped out of college after her father was diagnosed with cancer, and made a series of false starts while figuring out what to do with her life. Then she traveled to New York to visit a cousin and fell in love with the Big Apple. One morning, she took a bus tour past the New York Stock Exchange and decided *This is what I'm going to do with myself.* When she applied for a position with Merrill Lynch, though, she was told that she could never be hired without a college degree – and that she would hear the same thing everywhere she applied.

Someone else might have accepted that. Muriel's desire to work in New York's financial market, though, was strong enough to overcome the negative advice handed out by "experts." With gumption and intelligent risk-taking, she was eventually hired by one of the smaller firms – and gradually began to establish herself taking stock orders on the Street. In 1967, she became the first female member of the New York Stock Exchange. Two years later, she started Muriel Siebert & Co., Inc., the first female-operated firm on the NYSE. Today she's known as "The First Woman of Finance."

My late friend Catherine Shouse also comes to mind when I think of rutbusters. Kay was a woman who never settled down for long – although she could have done so many times in her life. Early on, Kay developed the habit of breaking rules – and she perfected it over a lifetime. She was the first woman to receive a M.Ed. degree from Harvard University and later was appointed to women's rights commissions by Presidents Kennedy, Nixon, Ford and Reagan. She was an author, an activist, a philanthropist and a humanitarian. At an age when other women would have disappeared into retirement, Kay launched the project that she is best known for – the world-renowned Wolf Trap Farm Park outside of Washington. In the last years of her life, Kay became involved with our arts center here in Florida. I was visiting with her not long before she died when Kay said something I'll never forget: "Don't ever give up something important if you believe in it. Not only will you regret it, but you will deny other people."

When I hear people say they are "too old" to start over again, I think of Lindy Boggs, whom I visited in Rome a number of years ago. Offered the post of ambassador to the Vatican at age 83, she didn't give it a second thought. Lindy epitomizes what I think of as one of the most important, but elusive, traits of a rutbuster: Giving back – the white magic I spoke of earlier. In a sense, Lindy's life can be summed up by one question, a question she has never stopped asking: What can I do to help? Ask yourself this question enough and you will be surprised how it changes your life.

Nowadays, I sometimes give talks on "rutbusting," explaining some of the traits that make a rutbuster. But there's no need for it to seem complicated. Rutbusting is simply breaking the habits that keep us from our potentials. We can't all be Edward Villellas or Muriel Sieberts or Catherine Shouses or Lindy Boggses. But we can learn and draw inspiration from their examples.

By 1965, I was engaged to a man who lived in Washington, D.C., the self-made head of a major national newspaper-radio operation. He was a fun man. I wore his ring and expected to move East and be married to him one day. But I kept putting him off while I worked to establish myself in the advertising world; I wanted to make sure Roche, Rickard, Henri, Hurst, Inc. was on the right course first. At least that was the excuse I gave myself.

My goal was to eventually move to New York and work on Madison Avenue, perhaps for Doyle Dane Bernbach.

But instead, two things happened to me that changed my life. The first – winning Advertising Woman of the Year – I've already told you about. The second turned out to have a more dramatic – and long-lasting – impact.

FIVE

Merger

had known the name Draper Daniels for some time, although it wasn't until 1965 that I got to know him. By then, he was considered something of a legend in the advertising world, having created such campaigns as the Marlboro Man while executive vice president at the Leo Burnett Company. In the 1950s, Dan had been the top creative man at Leo Burnett, but he left advertising to take a job in the Kennedy Administration's Department of Commerce.

There was speculation for a while that he might enter politics himself, to run against Everett Dirksen for the U.S. Senate from Illinois. But after the Kennedy assassination in November of 1963, he returned to advertising, and to Chicago, becoming executive vice president of McCann-Erickson, in charge of worldwide creative. Rumors circulated that he wasn't happy there, though, and wanted his own company.

I was introduced to Draper Daniels by Vivian Hill, a stylish, intelligent woman who dressed in Chanel suits and high heels and wore the most gorgeous South Seas pearls I'd ever seen. Vivian was a headhunter, whose specialty was bringing corporations together. We used to have lunch every two weeks, sharing the latest news and gossip about the advertising business. It was over one of these lunches that she mentioned that Draper Daniels might be interested in purchasing our company.

Our company was on-the-grow at this time, but something was holding us back – we needed a top-of-the-line creative director. When Vivian told me about Draper Daniels, I thought he might just be the ticket. I also figured I could probably learn a great deal about the business by working with him. Vivian offered to call Draper Daniels and say I was interested. He agreed to come in the next day at 5 p.m. and meet with me.

Draper Daniels was a tall, distinguished-looking man, who was known as a maverick – and also as something of a chauvinist. When he walked in the office at Roche, Rickard, Henri, Hurst, Inc., heads turned. "Is that Draper Daniels?" people whispered.

The first thing he did when he came into my office was kick the antique desk, which I thought a little odd. I remember thinking, *He's not only a chauvinist, he's also a klutz* (both perceptions, it turned out, were wrong). Then he sat down across from me and said, "Miss Janco, I'm so glad to meet you. Now tell me: What do you think is the best advertising in America right now and why?"

I reluctantly answered his questions, only to find that he had others. Question after question, until it began to feel more like an interrogation than a business meeting.

Finally, after close to an hour, I said, "Mr. Daniels, you came here to investigate a business and you haven't asked one question about that business."

"But if I buy a business I'm also buying the head of the company to run it," he replied.

So he kept asking questions – not the ones I expected. He never even asked to look at our books. What really interested Dan, I came to realize, was not sales volume, it was vision. He wanted to understand my ideas about how we could stand out above the other agencies. So I told him some of my ideas: I thought we could service national accounts with a kind of individual attention that the bigger agencies weren't able to provide, for example. I proposed taking some of our fees in stock from our clients' businesses, to show how committed we were to the product and how concerned we were about volume. He liked those ideas.

Finally, at about ten o'clock that night – he'd come in the office at five fifteen – Draper Daniels said, "Miss Janco, you must be hungry. Do you want to go get a hamburger?" So we walked down to the Wrigley Building and we had a couple of their famous hamburgers. We talked a little more and then he told me that he wanted to buy the business. He also said that he wanted me to stay. I told him I couldn't – that I was planning to move to New York. "But I'll stay long enough for you to feel comfortable running the company," I told him.

A few minutes later, he said: "If I were to do this, what would we name the company?"

"Well, the best name in the business is Draper Daniels, so maybe we should call it that." All the way home, I was mad at myself for handing him the name so easily.

The next day, Dan – which is what he called himself – phoned Vivian. He wanted to make the deal. I said, "Would you like your lawyer and finance man to come and meet with me and my finance man?" He said, "No. It's not necessary. You have an honest face. Whatever you want for the business will be fine."

A few days later he ended up writing a check for the business – paying two and a half times its face value. I kept my stock in the company, which was 24.5 percent, and Draper Daniels bought everything else. He wanted to come in as CEO and wanted me to be COO and president, which meant I would oversee the hands-on operation of the company. He also wanted a new board of directors.

The next day we held a press conference to announce that Draper Daniels was taking over the company. The most memorable part of it was that he introduced me as "Myrna Junko." George Lazarus, who was then a business editor at the *Chicago Tribune*, leaned over to me at that point and said, "Myra, how well do you know this fellow?" I later learned that his favorite bird was the dark-eyed junko and his favorite actress was Myrna Loy, so maybe that had something to do with it. It was, at any rate, one of many unexpected moments from Draper Daniels.

Standing Out

The company grew and changed under Draper Daniels. We landed pieces of several major accounts – Colgate-Palmolive, Swift, Speed Queen, Motorola, Consolidated Foods. When the John Hancock Building opened in 1966, we took over the twenty-fifth and twenty-seventh floors – a nice, comfortable work space with a splendid view of Chicago.

Dan was, in effect, the creative director of the company and I was the marketing director. All of the finance and account people reported to me. It was a good fit.

One of the things that made our agency different from other firms was that we hired several of the best creative leaders in the business to work for us. Men like Ernie Evers, who had done the Dial In, Dial Out campaign for Dial and was head of creative at Foote, Cone & Belding, and John Matthew, who had created Tony the Tiger. No other firm in the industry had as many proven creative minds as we did. We got them because they wanted to work with Dan; they came to us, we didn't have to go shopping for them.

Our agency deliberately tried to be a little different. We didn't watch the clock the way most firms did and we never charged for copy. We did a lot of single-fee accounts and took nothing that would bring us less than a quarter of a million dollars net. We weren't the largest advertising agency – we had about seventy-five employees – but we were one of the best, a boutique agency with a solid list of clients. And in a sense, we were doing what Dan and I had talked about in our first conversation – providing services and creative campaigns that no other company could provide.

I learned a lot from Draper Daniels. He wasn't a great businessman but he was a brilliant wordsmith, who taught me to state my ideas clearly and concisely, as if I was talking to one person. That was his philosophy: Talk to one person. He was a man who was interested in creativity for creativity's sake. Dan never stopped being a copywriter. That was his true passion. His campaigns were simple but brilliant. I'll never forget his Campbell's Tomato Soup Quality Campaign. You could almost literally smell the soup pouring.

Dan enjoyed the work, but he knew how to have fun – more than I did. He had a wonderful, contagious sense of humor and a boyish, mischievous quality; often, it was hard to tell when he was serious and when he was joking. He also knew how to relax. He would often be off swimming or playing handball by six o'clock while I would still be at the office sometimes until eleven o'clock or midnight.

I stayed in Chicago much longer than I expected because it was difficult to leave a job that taught me so much and was also so stimulating.

A Proposal

One day, after he had been with the firm for about two years, Dan came into my office with a card in his hand. By this time, the firm had been through several buyouts and mergers and I had a funny feeling that he was about to tell me of another one. I said to him, "What are you doing now? Are you going to sell *me* with the next merger?"

"Not exactly," he said.

He had written out a list of his own best personal character traits on the card. On the other side, he had written out mine. I thought, *What in the world has gotten into him?* But I said, "It sounds like another merger to me, and it sounds like you're trying to sell yourself, too."

"No, not exactly," he said. "I've been thinking about this for nine months, Myra, and I think we would make a great team."

I said, "I think we *are* a great team. Think of what we've accomplished so far this year."

He said, "I'm talking about a different sort of merger."

"Oh."

"Yes, I've decided I'd like to marry you."

I lost my voice for a moment, because I had never thought of the man that way – and had no idea he had thought of me that way. Dan was twelve and a half years older than me, and had been married before. I was against divorce in those days. But more importantly, I was happy with my life. I told him that.

"All right," he said. "Let's talk about it again tomorrow." And then he walked out whistling – which is, to me, one of the most maddening things anyone can do, and even more so under the circumstances.

I had a meeting that afternoon on an account that brought in twenty three million dollars a year. But I called to say I'd be a few minutes late. I went home first and called Len, my fiancé, back in Washington. I told him what Dan had just said.

Len knew of Draper and he just laughed. "Come on," he said. "He's pulling your leg."

I returned to the office and told Dan, "Merger accepted in fifteen years. Today, let's get some new business."

Well, Dan came down from his office on the double, carrying a Peacock Jewelers ring box. "Don't be ridiculous," I said. "Put that in the safe. I couldn't even think about marrying someone without a year's courtship."

"All right," he said, "we'll count today as day one, then." And he put out his hand and we shook, as if sealing a business proposition.

We went out to dinner that night, which was the first time I really got to know Dan as a person. He was very funny and charismatic but also much more down to earth than I had thought. Dan hailed from a Quaker family in a small upstate New York town and never forgot his roots. His father had been a civil engineer who helped navigate the Alaska inland passage; his mother also came from Quaker parents. Draper was his mother's family name, but he thought it made him sound like a sissy so he had adopted the name Dan. His mother called him "D." When Dan was a boy, his family struggled to pay the bills; years later, after he became the highest paid advertising man in the country, he bought his mother a fabulous diamond ring and told her that it was the ring his father had wanted to buy her but could never afford.

Dan was a restless man who loved the creative side of advertising, but not the business side. He enjoyed nothing more than giving birth to an idea. Ironically, he had been behind several of the best known cigarette campaigns, but he had left the ad business to join the Kennedy administration, he said, because he was bothered about promoting a product that was being linked to cancer.

I learned a lot about Dan that night and saw sides of him I hadn't known before. Afterward, he drove me home, parked in the drive, and said he wanted to come in and tell Aunt Goldie the news.

"*What* news?" I said. "There's nothing to tell."

He said, "That you and I have a yearlong courtship. Shouldn't she know?"

I told him no. But Dan was determined, as he often was, so he came in and told her. Goldie fixed him with her bright blue eyes and said, "Draper, you're much too old and slightly soiled for her. It would never last more than six months." And then she turned to me and said that rather than watch us makes fools of ourselves, she was going to move back to Indiana – which she did, before the week was out.

When my fiancé realized that Dan was serious, he flew right out to Chicago to see me. I asked him for a year's sabbatical. He was furious, and said what Goldie had said – that it would never last.

Well, it turned out Dan wasn't too old and he wasn't too soiled. And despite my resolve, the "merger" occurred about six weeks later.

We had a mutual friend at the time, who was a medical doctor, and one day she invited us over to her house for a Sunday brunch. She insisted that we not eat anything before we came over, which seemed odd. The first thing she did when we arrived at her apartment was take blood samples. This made me a little mad. I said, "Dan, we've got a year to think about whether we want to have a blood test"; but, for some reason, I went along with it.

After Aunt Goldie moved away, I sold my large, colonial house in Evanston and moved into an apartment hotel downtown. Dan was living in town, too, and we began to see each other in the evenings, often for dinner. Shortly after this Sunday brunch, I mentioned to him that I was planning to go to an Edna Arnow pottery show on Saturday; Dan said he wanted to come with me.

I remember telling him that same night how much I enjoyed living by myself. *It's so nice to not always have to worry about what another person is doing or thinking*, I told him.

"Mmm hmm," he said.

The next day, August 19, 1967, he picked me up to go to the pottery show. He asked if he could stop for a minute at the courthouse. I told him okay, I would wait in the car while he went inside and conducted his business. He said, "I can't leave you alone in the car in this neighborhood. Won't you just come along?" So I did, and we got off at a floor with a sign that read "Marriage Licenses." I had assumed for some reason that he was at the courthouse for a fishing license.

"Myra," he said, "I'm not getting any younger and I think we should get a license."

"But we have a year."

He just looked at me. I went up to the clerk at the counter and said, "We're not getting married. We have a year to wait. If we got a license, this wouldn't be published, would it?" The clerk said, "If you request that it not be published, no, it won't." So that's what we did. But it didn't matter. There was an office across the hall where marriages were performed and Dan said to me, "Myra, let's go ahead and do it." I couldn't speak. But the next thing I knew, I had done it. We were married. And I started to cry.

On Monday, Dan called a meeting at the office. The funny thing was that nobody in our company knew of the engagement – or even that we were seeing each other. Dan called all the employees together and announced that there had been another merger. Then he said, "Myra and I were married this weekend."

Our staff was a little shell-shocked. The headline in the newspaper the next day was: "Another Merger at Draper Daniels."

About two weeks later, we honeymooned in the Bahamas, which was where Dan showed me how to fish and I caught my first big wahoo. Looking back now, I realize I never regretted for a moment marrying him. But I resisted pretty strongly at first. I think it shows that sometimes we don't know what's best for ourselves. I had been so work-oriented and had resisted so much that Dan pursued me. I'm grateful that he did. I trace my stubbornness to my grandmother who had told me I should never kiss a boy on the lips. If I had followed her advice, I'd never have married Dan.

We lived a good life. We had a spectacular apartment in Chicago and bought a working farm ninety-seven miles away. The farm was right near Ronald Reagan's hometown of Dixon and if you walked around the square back then, everybody, it seemed, looked like Ronald Reagan.

Years later in Florida, after Dan lost his battle with cancer, I was cleaning out his old highboy chest and I found two rolls of nickels in a drawer. I had no idea what they were doing there – but I thought immediately of Vivian Hill, the woman who had introduced us back in 1965. I remembered how Vivian used to keep these rolls of nickels lined up in the crevices of her roll-top desk drawer and would often make bets with people. She'd say things like, "I'll bet you two rolls of nickels that Procter and Gamble is going to move from this agency to that agency." I was still in touch with her so I rang her up and said, "Vivian, the strangest thing happened. I opened up the drawer to Dan's old highboy and I found two rolls of nickels, like I would sometimes win from you." And she started laughing.

I said, "Why are you laughing?"

"Didn't he ever tell you?"

"Tell me what?"

So Vivian told me a little story about Dan that I didn't know: The morning after I had met Dan in 1965 – the night we talked for five hours, then went out for hamburgers at the Wrigley building – he had gone to visit Vivian, and said he wanted to buy the company. I knew that part, but I didn't know what came next. He also said to her, "Vivian, just for your information, within two years that woman is going to be Mrs. Daniels." She bet him two rolls of nickels that he was wrong. The day after we were married, in 1967, she had paid him.

Dan kept the nickels.

SIX

Selling Dreams

"There is nothing like a dream to create the future." –Victor Hugo

Retirement, I have always believed, is highly overrated. It's also unnatural. Too many people retire and then find themselves at loose ends, wondering what to do. I have seen this happen over and over again, particularly here in Florida, where so many people go to pasture in their later years. Those who continue to challenge themselves are healthier and happier than those who completely retire and fall asleep.

I believed this before I retired and I believe it much more strongly now – twenty-some years after "un-retiring." But when you are married, you make decisions together and often they involve compromise. By 1979, my husband wanted to leave the world of advertising and live a different life. I understood why, even as part of me resisted. He was tired of going into the office every day. He also didn't like the direction the advertising business was going. This was a time when conglomerates were buying up the smaller agencies, and individual creative mavericks were out of fashion. The nature of advertising had changed, too: this was an era of experimental campaigns, when advertisers had begun talking about their competitors by name – a longtime no-no in advertising circles. Dan thought that the basics of advertising were being lost.

I was still in my prime, though, and didn't want to retire. But I did want to keep my husband. Dan envisioned a life where he could go out to the farm and travel and fish. He had also begun to write a novel, the story of a farm boy who goes to Washington and becomes a political leader. It was based, in part, on his work with the Kennedy administration.

Dan had been smitten with Southwest Florida ever since we first visited in the winter of 1971. The occasion was a national sales meeting for Colgate-Palmolive. We had just won part of the Colgate-Palmolive account and were scheduled to make a presentation to the C-P sales force at a meeting at the Fontainebleau in Miami Beach.

The week before the meeting, Dan came into my office and told me he had just read in the paper that "the snook are running" in a little place called Marco Island. "Oh? That's nice," I told him. "What does that mean?"

Dan, who had never caught a snook, said, "Say, Myra, let's go down a day early. I want to catch some snook."

"Are you crazy?" I said. "This is our first national meeting with the sales staff. We have to sell these people. I have too much on my mind."

He said, "Oh Myra, we'll do fine."

So I sat in the back of a rental car with a pencil, working on my script, as Dan drove us to Marco Island to fish for snook. I was terribly disinterested. But Dan was an avid fisherman and he fell in love with this largely undeveloped jewel. Home prices were ridiculously low then, so it wasn't long before he bought a lot.

Eight years later, he convinced me to leave our Chicago condominium behind and move permanently to this sleepy residential community in Florida where the snook were still running.

Retirement was an adjustment for me. In Chicago, we had lived at Water Tower Place in the heart of the city, across the street from the John Hancock Building. Out on Marco Island, our house was dozens of miles from a major shopping center. It was hard to even get a housekeeper, so I had a lot of time for thinking while I swept the porch, vacuumed and dusted.

Our life was much simpler on Marco. I kept busy cooking and painting. Dan fished and wrote his novel. Sometimes I would go for long walks and talk to the dolphins. This was when it really began to strike me how unnatural retirement was. It was disturbing to meet so many talented, intelligent and creative people who were spending their days watching television, playing cards and fishing. This was the time of life when we finally had the freedom to do what we wanted and so many of us were doing nothing. Retirement seemed like a self-imposed prison in some ways; I was glad that Dan seemed happy, but I knew that eventually I would have to find something to do with myself.

A few months after our retirement, Aunt Goldie fell and broke her hip. I flew up to Indiana to visit with her in the hospital. Despite her initial disapproval of my relationship with Dan, we had stayed close. Now in her late eighties, Goldie was still an inspiration to me, writing each day, sometimes selling her work to the *Chicago Tribune* and the *Christian Science Monitor*.

I wasn't in Indiana more than twenty minutes when the telephone rang. It was Dan.

"You need to come home," he said. "We have a problem."

I said, "With the cats?"

He said, "No. Just the big cat. I want to talk to you directly," he said, "not over the phone."

I didn't know what to think. I was pretty certain he wasn't going to tell me he had another babe stashed away. And Dan always seemed the picture of health – I couldn't imagine he was ill. What I didn't realize was that he had been having a problem for a while and the minute I got out of town, he went to his doctor to be tested.

So I flew back and he told me he had cancer. "I have to go in for an operation immediately."

I was too green to feel fear. I thought we were going to lick this together. I thought the cancer was just an enemy that could be defeated. But it kept coming back. He ended up having five operations over the next four years. Between them, he would seem to get better, then we'd receive the bad news. The last operation was at Sloan-Kettering in New York. It was a seven-and-a-half-hour procedure. When the doctor came out, I knew we were in trouble.

Dan eventually came home and died in Southwest Florida. He never got to finish his novel. His four children came to stay with us before he died, and for a week afterward. It was not an unhappy time. We fished his favorite spots and told Dan stories and it felt at times as if we were all a family.

Getting Lost

After everyone left, though, I didn't know what to do. While Dan was ill in Florida, Goldie had died in Indiana. Within a year, the two most important people in my life were gone. I thought for a while that I would go back to Chicago and return to work – although I couldn't work in my field because of a buy/sell agreement I had signed. Without Dan, I just didn't want to be retired.

During my long walks on the beach, a question kept coming to me: *What can I do to make my world a better place?* For a long time, I didn't know. What I did know was that I didn't want to sit around and feel sorry for myself. I also didn't want to spend my days playing bridge or golfing.

For weeks, I took walks and became lost in my thoughts. I placed my faith in a higher power and eventually found an answer to my question.

While Dan was sick, I had received a call one night from two women who wanted to form a chamber music ensemble on Marco Island. Our community was very remote, a couple of hours from Miami, and this was both a blessing and a curse. There was lots of natural beauty where we lived – miles of gorgeous unspoiled beaches and waterways – but virtually none of the cultural beauty – music, art and theater – found in metropolitan areas. But I began to realize, slowly, that there was plenty of hunger for it.

These two women knew that I was from Chicago and that I had an interest in music. They asked if I could help them. At the time, I told them I couldn't really do much. But shortly after Dan died, I went around to see this fledgling chamber group perform at a local church. It was really just a little pick-up orchestra, in need of rehearsing; but I remember sitting there in church and thinking, *This is a good thing. This is what the community needs.* So I decided to support it.

But they sorely needed leadership – and a plan. I told them that to make this work, we had to approach it as a business. First, we needed a budget.

What sort of a budget? they asked.

I suggested a goal of $100,000, which would enable the chamber orchestra to perform four concerts a year. I think they thought I was crazy. But I went home and paged through the phone book, marking every few residential numbers with a red dot and then began to make calls. To each of the respondents I explained that we were building an orchestra that would perform in our community; I then asked if they would like to join us. The community was even hungrier than I had imagined. It took only five days to raise the hundred thousand dollars.

The turning point came when I called a woman named Frances Hayes. I gave her my line about building an orchestra and she said, "Well, that's a wonderful idea." We chatted for a while and I asked her what part of the world she was from. "Philadelphia," she said. I told her that my mother used to take me to Philadelphia to hear the orchestra.

"Oh," she said. "My father was their biggest donor."

Her father, she added, was J. Howard Pew, one of the founders of the Pew Charitable Trust and president of Sun Oil Company. We had a nice conversation about music and culture, although at the end of it she said, "Unfortunately, we've given all our money away for this year. But I can give you twenty-five."

That was fine with me. Each contribution, large or small, was a step in the right direction. When I got to Mrs. Hayes' house the next day to pick up her check, I found what she had meant by "twenty-five." Her check was written out for $25,000.

It grew from there. We started by selling a dream, and soon, as the money came in and we began to build a quality orchestra, we shared one.

There were many other happy surprises in the months ahead. One woman donated lodging for musicians, enabling us to hire musicians from the East Coast. Then I received a call one day from Jerome Hines, who owned a lot on Marco Island. He had read an article in the newspaper about this woman who was building an orchestra, and he offered to perform a recital benefit for us at a local country club. My friend and state legislator Mary Ellen Hawkins led the charge for government funding.

The theme of our campaign became, *If you want great music in your life, join us. Together, we will build this.*

I never planned to be on the orchestra's board; I just wanted to help them get organized. But the shared excitement of what we were doing made it impossible to quit. Fundraising became an obsession with me. It was fun, and contagious, to once again build something from nothing.

Once we had a financial base, we concentrated on the product. We needed better players, and so began holding auditions in Miami. More importantly, we needed a conductor, an experienced maestro who could lead the orchestra and help it grow. One of my heroes growing up had been Walter Hendel, who was then associate conductor of the Chicago Symphony; Maestro Hendel had done all the children's concerts in Chicago. Later, he was the music director of the Dallas Symphony. I flew out to see him conduct in Dallas and, afterward, went backstage and asked if he'd come to Marco and do four concerts a year for us.

He said yes, agreeing on a salary of $10,000 per concert. Eventually, Walter steered us to a young man named Tim Russell, who was studying to be a music teacher. Tim became our first music director. A few years later, we replaced Tim

Get Lost

Being able to change perspective is one of the most valuable, but neglected, aspects of success. I do this by periodically "getting lost."

Getting lost means escaping from yourself, wandering away from your day-to-day routines, taking a vacation from your problems, your illusions, your fears. Getting lost inspires and replenishes. It can also be an effective means of problem-solving: Take a break, do something completely different – plant a garden, walk along the water, prepare a three-course dinner, go for a rambling drive – and let your subconscious mind go to work. When you return to the problem, it will invariably look different.

Getting lost also allows us to find surprising moments of wonder and beauty that we wouldn't ordinarily notice – the glitter of sun sequins on a marshy creek, the silhouette of oak trees in an evening sky, the wide, questing eyes of a child.

Getting lost is often the best way of really finding ourselves.

with Christopher Seaman, one of Britain's leading conductors, and Erich Kunzel, the world's most renowned pops conductor at the time. It still amazes me how much this orchestra has accomplished in such a short time. By the mid-1990s, the Naples Philharmonic Orchestra, as it is now known, was nationally recognized. We had appeared on two PBS specials, accompanied such renowned singers as Luciano Pavarotti, Dmitri Hvorostovsky, Dame Kiri Te Kanawa and Frederica von Stade and had been nominated for a Grammy Award. It was a lot of work, but it never seemed like work. People cared and people shared. They wanted to be a part of our family. That was the most effective selling point, and one of the secrets of our success: We became a family.

Making Culture Contagious

It was Frances Pew Hayes who told me that we shouldn't just build an orchestra, we should also build a home for that orchestra. At the time she told me this, I wondered if we were ready for that. "Maybe not," Mrs. Hayes said, "but if I know you, someday this will be a first-rate orchestra and then there won't be any land left. In fact, let me give you $2 million to get started."

I told her, "Mrs. Hayes, we appreciate your offer. But we don't even have a plan yet. However, if you agree to put your money in escrow and give me six months, we *will* have a plan."

That's how the orchestra fundraising drive became the drive to build an arts center. The community was even more excited by the plan for a performing arts center than they were about the orchestra. In fact, there was another group in town that also wanted to build an arts center and we became opponents. For several years, they fought us tooth and nail. But by the time we ran into them head-on, we already had $9 million.

Fundraising became my full-time job. I can't even say for sure when this other group gave up. I just stopped paying attention and eventually they went away. We rented a small office on the highway where I set up green theater seats – just like what we'd have in the hall. People would come in and I'd sell them a seat in the theater. We literally sold the arts center to the community. Every hallway, seat, piece of carpet and brick was sponsored by donation – everything except the urinals. Contributions ranged from several million dollars to the $1.29 offered by a young boy to buy a $100 brick (I accepted the offer but gave the boy back a dime after he told me it was his entire savings). One woman pledged ten dollars from her monthly Social Security check. "Best damn project I ever saw!" she told me on Opening Night as she rode up on her bicycle. To date, more than seventy thousand people have contributed to the center.

Along the way, the concept of the arts center evolved with the enthusiasm of the community – from a home for the orchestra to a full-scale performing arts complex that would also encompass world-class visual arts.

Once we decided to build the Philharmonic Center, I talked with ten architects, all of whom told me we shouldn't have art galleries in the hall. I thought, *What do people do during intermission?* Our region didn't yet have an art museum and I knew people were hungry for art. Why can't we also offer museum quality exhibitions?

After some deliberation, I finally settled on Eugene Aubry, who had recently designed the Wortham Theater in Houston. Gene didn't think art galleries fit with a performing arts center, either. So I told him, "Gene, we'll pay for it, you do it."

Ten years later, the community's support enabled us to build a three-story art museum adjacent to our center. One of the characteristics that has set us apart from other arts complexes is our mission of combining all of the arts – performing as well as visual – in a single complex under a single management.

On November 3, 1989, the Philharmonic Center for the Arts opened, 95 percent debt-free. Soon afterward, we were 100 percent debt-free. The center has steadily grown since then, both artistically and fiscally. Today, we are a $105 million nonprofit corporation – and an example of how a community can build something from nothing.

Why did it work? First, because we believed in what we were doing and used that belief as a tool to create what some thought was not possible. Second, because we applied the principles of business to our efforts. Too many performing arts organizations put the arts first, business second. That's not a recipe for success or survival. From the beginning, when we made those fundraising calls for the orchestra, we approached this as a business – with an organized business plan and specific goals. There's no reason why show business can't also be good business. But culture does not convert to cash without careful planning. A performing arts hall has to be conceived, planned and built under the rigid disciplines one would apply in starting any new company.

Why have we remained successful when so many arts centers and orchestras are operating at a loss? One important reason is that we have stayed in sync with our changing community. The challenge is not so much building an arts center as sustaining the community's interest. Once built, performing arts centers have an enormous capacity to lose money. Because we shared the building of this arts center with the community, there is a feeling of ownership that some other arts organizations don't have. Together, we changed the cultural flavor of a sleepy seaside community, and showed that the arts can be alive and kicking in small-town America. This arts center is a monument to that effort; it belongs to the community.

We have also tapped an important resource too often overlooked. There are many retired corporate officers in Florida playing golf or lying in the sun, bored and restless. Our board includes retired CEOs from some of the largest companies in the country. One result of their pragmatism was the establishment, early on, of an endowment fund that will be a life-sustaining factor for our future. There is a tremendous need in the arts world for the talents and connections that these former executives have developed in their business careers.

We continue to grow by working together and paying attention. Part of our mission is to bring the arts to everyone – to reach out to children, and to reach out to the underprivileged. The arts aren't elitist, although they sometimes carry that stigma. To me, one of the most gratifying sights is the look of wonder in a young child's eyes when he or she experiences a classical music or dance performance for the first time. Youth programs are a major component of the Philharmonic Center. Our future, I sometimes say, is in the little hands of our children.

The Philharmonic Center hasn't "ruined" the community, as some people had warned early on. But the impact of world-class cultural opportunities has certainly changed it. Naples Mayor Bill Barnett was recently asked what effect the Philharmonic Center has had on the city and the region. "It's done two things," he replied. "It established Naples at a national level and it set a new standard for excellence that can be felt in every part of the community."

The Philharmonic Center is an example of what a community can accomplish when it is galvanized, and it shares a belief. Our arts complex belongs to the people of Southwest Florida and will serve this now culturally savvy community for generations to come.

As my grandmother Sophie said when I was four years old, and about to launch my first business: "Create something that people want and need." This is what we have done.

SEVEN

What I've Learned

"To accomplish great things, we must not only act but also dream, not only plan but also believe." – Anatole France

"The art of being wise is the art of knowing what to overlook." – William James

When I was young, I often sought out older people for what they could teach me – because they had done things I hadn't done and knew things I didn't know. I still believe in surrounding myself with those who have skills and knowledge I don't have. That's part of the adventure of learning.

On the other hand, I've come to increasingly rely on my own instincts and passions and to redefine some of the concepts that tend to be our biggest stumbling blocks – success, failure, risk-taking, salesmanship. I've learned that it's important not to accept what we're expected to accept, but to go a little deeper, to question widely held assumptions. Alexander Pope had a good line – "Some people will never learn anything for this reason, because they understand everything too soon." Don't understand things too soon. Learn to find your own way.

I recall something the great abstract artist Jules Olitski shared with us when he brought his retrospective to our arts center several years ago. Olitski recounted how, when he was thirteen years old, he attended the funeral of his grandmother and had a "vision": "It was a gray, drizzly day and I just had this thought standing in the rain, this feeling that there has to be more to life than the way we're living," he recalled. "And I remember thinking, as my grandmother was lowered into the grave and dirt was dropped on her, that if there is something in me that means anything, that is real, then I must pursue it. And I knew that it was making art. I had no idea why or what it meant other than this feeling that art could be a life with a higher purpose."

Years later, Olitski was a struggling artist living in Paris, painting in a formal style, frustrated with the direction in which his life and his work were going. "I was alone in the apartment one day," he said, "and I looked at what I was doing and thought, 'What's going on? What happened to the graveside thing, the vision?' And I thought the only way to find out would be to let those feelings come out again, to just paint what I felt and let that child come out again. So what I did was I wrapped a towel around my head so I couldn't see and spread some paint out on a big plank of wood. I kind of knew where the colors were, and I began daubing at the canvas. When I was done, it looked pretty lively.

"I did it again the next day and again for a while. It never occurred to me that this was art but these paintings began to look fresh and exciting. And after some weeks, I thought, I can continue from here and I don't need this towel anymore. And that's how I started painting abstract art."

It was with these so-called "blindfold paintings" that Jules Olitski began to find his identity as an artist, and his path as a person. What he was describing is a form of "rutbusting" – of changing perspective to change your life; of making a little adjustment to bring about a big difference.

When people think they need to make a *big change* in their lives, what they really mean is they need to do something that will make a *big difference*. Often, the change that can make that big difference is very small – decide to exercise for twenty minutes each morning, for instance, instead of watching television. By thinking about change but not making it, we empower it. Change becomes CHANGE. Ruts make us comfortable, not happy. The longer we stay in them, the more they control and distort our judgment.

From childhood on, most of us are fed illusory, ultimately limiting, ideas about who we are and how we should lead our lives. Some of these we feed ourselves. Confidence and belief must be coupled with a search for the truth, I believe, in order for us to advance and succeed. We can't follow someone else's map to find ourselves or to find success. But if you hear something more than two or three times that is at odds with what you believe, pay attention. Periodically take a disgustingly honest look at yourself. Seek out the truth.

Here, again, are the eight lessons discussed in these pages, the "Secrets of a Rutbuster":

1. **Savor the Adventure of Being Different**
2. **Master the Art of Giving**
3. **Surround Yourself with Teachers**
4. **Find What You Love – And Do It!**
5. **Learn to Take Intelligent Risks**
6. **Go Back to School**
7. **Redefine Failure**
8. **Get Lost**

Giving Back

Every private citizen has a public responsibility. This became my creed as we began to envision an arts center for Southwest Florida – and as I realized that "retirement" was not what it's cracked up to be.

We all have to weigh our own private time against the time we give to our community. Everyone is part of a community. Each of us has individual talents, ideas and beliefs that can make the community a better place for all. Accept this responsibility and give to the greater good. You will be rewarded in ways you haven't imagined.

Acknowledgments

I am grateful to many friends and fellow rutbusters who were instrumental in shaping this story. In particular, I thank Jim Lilliefors, who for eight years has encouraged, nudged and helped me.

I also wish to thank Dianne Sponseller for her invaluable assistance.

DISCOVER YOUR PASSIONS **DREAM**

LEARN SOMETHING NEW EVERY DAY Organize

Be Different *Make Things Happen*

GET LOST REDEFINE FAILURE

DISCOVER YOUR PASSIONS **DREAM**

LEARN SOMETHING NEW EVERY DAY Organize

Be Different *Make Things Happen*

GET LOST REDEFINE FAILURE

DISCOVER YOUR PASSIONS **DREAM**

LEARN SOMETHING NEW EVERY DAY Organize

Be Different *Make Things Happen*

GET LOST REDEFINE FAILURE

DISCOVER YOUR PASSIONS **DREAM**

LEARN SOMETHING NEW EVERY DAY Organize

Be Different *Make Things Happen*

GET LOST REDEFINE FAILURE